Mortified:
A Motherhood
Memoir

Keelan LaForge

ISBN: 9798358594890

Credits for Cover – james@goonwrite.com
Printed in Belfast, United Kingdom.
Publisher – Independently Published

Chapter One – Jumping into the Pool

People say that having kids keeps you young. I don't know who came up with that saying, but it must have been a babysitter that was clocking out at nine PM with a hefty wad of bank notes in their hand. It definitely wasn't someone that was actively parenting every minute of their lives – unless they were too far gone on certain substances to really know what they were doing. Having kids is rewarding and magical and all those other highly emotive words, but it hasn't done my complexion any favours. I have acquired many new facial lines, and the V between my eyebrows is much more pronounced than my laughter lines are now. I jest – sort of. My kids make me laugh all the time. Their ridiculous and hilarious antics brighten every day and make me thankful I chose chaos over free time and attractive décor any day. But sometimes they drive you to the brink of madness.

I couldn't have anticipated what it would be like. I thought having a child would be like having a cuddlier cat. My sister said the same. She's now had a reality check three times over. If I'm honest, I never really pictured my kids beyond the baby stage. Maybe that was short-sighted of me, or maybe it's just a self-preservation thing. Everyone must envisage the classic family portrait in their mind when they first plan to have kids. I don't think anyone daydreams about the meltdowns in the supermarket that turn you into a celebrity in your community for a day – not the kind of fame you would want.

Today, I took my kids to swimming lessons for the first time ever. My daughter was disgusted that she was forced to be in the bottom group, even though she can't swim yet. We haven't been swimming in a very long time. I suck at swimming, and I don't want my kids to be burdened with the same fear as me - of swimming in front of the lifeguard and not being able to complete a length. There have been times when it has happened – usually when I've forgotten to take my inhaler and I've been gasping for breath, like a fish out of water, only I'm in water and I'm a human out of air. I've just had to power through, hoping they won't have to perform a rescue, or at least toss me a float because they've spotted my swimming shortcomings. So, they've started lessons. I get to observe parts of the class from the café window. Most of the parents beat me to the front row, so I probably miss the best bits. At one point, I saw one of the swimming instructors watering the kids on the heads with a watering can. I thought it was a pretty funny way of getting them accustomed to having water in their eyes, but my kids didn't look impressed by it. Still, they're going back. If for no other reason than to hopefully get a full night's sleep thanks to the doggy paddle exhausting them.

I think they thought they'd be Olympic swimmers by the end of day one, but they're in a group with several other kids and from what I could see, they were all mostly thrashing around on floats and with pool noodles. They looked happy while they were doing it though – and they only got their faces dunked in the water a couple of times, so they weren't too traumatised by the end of it. There is already talk of the next visit lesson, which I think is a good sign.

Next time, I won't bother with the cup of coffee. The lesson is only thirty minutes long. By the time my coffee cooled enough to reach drinking temperature, it was time to pick them up again. I'd been quite pleased, if I'm honest, to pay for someone else to take my kids into the pool so I didn't have to get in. I do enjoy swimming – alone - but it's an ordeal when you're with your kids. You're basically just holding them in the water. You don't get a chance to do any real swimming of your own, which is probably a good thing if you swim like me. I want to be able to show my face there again. It's also the kind of place where I sense I'll run into someone I know every time we set foot in the place. At least yesterday, I ran into another mum I genuinely like. It could have been much more awkward than that. The café comprises about four tables, all facing the pool, so if you run into someone you don't love, you'll quickly be forced to get closer than you ever intended to.

I thought that because I wasn't going for a swim that I'd be spared getting wet and having to shower in one of the cubicles. I passed my kids their shower gel and shampoo, thinking it would be easier for them to have a quick shower while we were there, rather than having to embark on the arduous process of hair washing and styling after dinner at home. Of course, I was wrong. I always am when I expect something about motherhood to go smoothly. They both got shampoo in their eyes as soon as they applied it to their heads and came screeching at me at the same time, both demanding to have their eyes dried. They thought if they tipped their heads downwards when they stood under the shower it would prevent the water running into their eyes – instead it encouraged the shampoo to do it instead. After several attempts at drying their eyes and instructing them on how to shower without blinding themselves, I realised I'd have to get into the shower too. I was fully clothed and dry when I went in, shower sprayed and boot-soaked when I came out. Next time, I might have to wear a swimsuit just to get them ready to go home.

That's the only organised activity we are doing at the moment. My brain can't handle too much at once, and my daughter is getting violin lessons in school. Before I had kids, I thought if I gave them alliterative names, they'd maybe start a band when they were older. It had a ring to it – I thought it would be easier for people to remember, but everyone gets their names mixed up. When my immature, pre-kids mind conceived of my kids' stage names for later life, I didn't think of the post that would arrive, addressed to "Miss same first initial, same surname," and the fact that I'd never know whose letter it was until I opened it. I suppose that will worsen with age. For now, it's limited to doctor's letters and school notes. I used to think certain name choices were boring, but maybe people think they'll be easy to remember and prevent needless confusion. There is enough of that that comes with having children anyway.

Chapter Two - School Trip Shame

After accompanying my daughter on every school trip this year, I decided to give her a break and not sign up for the most recent one. I thought I was doing her a favour. The last two times, she scolded me for coming because I'd prevented her being paired with her best friend whose mum was also in attendance. If your mum was there, you got stuck in your mum's group, she said. It sounded like that struck horror into her heart.

They had been low-key outings. On two of them, we just had to walk to the nearest park for seasonal walks, and on another, we went to the local shops for the topic of "shopping" and some free cocktail sausages from the butcher. This trip was on a bus – a proper outing, and one you couldn't easily escape from if anything went awry.

When I told her I wasn't accompanying her that time, she sounded surprisingly disappointed.

"Oh, I thought you were coming," she said with little plaintive eyes.

"Oh, I will," I corrected myself. "I'll tell your teacher tomorrow."

I don't really have an excuse to get out of helping out – I'm at home writing every day anyway. If you ask most adults, that isn't considered real work anyway. It's like glorified thumb twiddling.

Truth be told, I was glad to be going on the trip with her. Even though I love getting a break when my kids are in school, I miss them too. I guess I'm so used to the madness, it feels eerily quiet when it comes to a complete stop.

About two months ago, we went to Rathlin Island for the first time. For anyone that doesn't live in Northern Ireland, it's the island where the puffins live, off the North Coast of Northern Ireland. When we arrived there and got off the ferry, we had to take a rickety bus to the bird centre. We drove on a road that wasn't made for traffic. It was both vertical and winding at the same time. The bus was rammed with people. It was a sunny day in April. That's practically unheard of in this country. Hence, everyone and their granny was out.

Since the bus was packed and it costs an extra five pounds for the kids to have their own seats, my boyfriend and I just held them on our knees. It was a bit ridiculous, considering one of them is eight and almost the same size as me, but it just seemed more economical and logical at the time. Anyway, the impact of that bus trip on them must have been greater than I thought.

On the morning of my daughter's school trip, we were walking to her school hand in hand. The sun was beaming down on us, and it felt like one of those picture-perfect mother-daughter moments. I was cherishing every moment spent together and the fact that there was no rush because I had nowhere else to be when she dropped the bomb on me.

"By the way, Mummy – I WILL NOT be sitting on your knee on the bus," she said, with the confidence of a key speaker.

I burst out laughing. Her comment was so much at odds with every aspect of that magical moment, and the way she said it was hilarious. At the age of nearly seven, I suppose the prospect of sitting on my knee in front of her friends was a step too far. I thought it was so funny that it was a real concern of hers. I had no intention of having her on my knee either, but it was funny that she found the idea of it so horrifying.

She agreed to be in my group for pond-dipping and seemed happy to have my company for the rest of the trip, once she'd asserted her independence where seating was concerned. I ended up sitting next to a little boy instead, since she abandoned me for her friends. It was hardly surprising, considering the fact she runs into her classroom most mornings without bothering to look back over her shoulder or say bye. But I'm glad I have such independent children. Yes, it's annoying sometimes – especially when I'm trying to persuade them to wear a pair of shoes that fits the occasion and location we are setting out to (outdoor activities on a flooded farm) and they want to wear something they had in mind (flip flops.) But I like that they're happy to strike out into the world and make their own way without tying themselves to my apron strings.

The wee boy I sat beside told me off before the bus even set off because I hadn't put my seatbelt on. When I was in school, there weren't any seatbelts on buses. We were lucky if we got a seat at all. I remember swinging around in the aisle, falling on top of other pupils whenever the driver came to a sudden stop. Once we went on a school trip and someone threw a rock through a window and the glass shattered over all of us. I thought about recounting that story, but I somehow felt that the humorous lack of safety would be lost on a child in 2022. He'd probably just tell me that the school should have put in a claim.

As I made idle conversation with the kid beside me, my daughter kept interjecting to shush me. I think she'd rather I hadn't spoken at all. I find it really funny when my kids are embarrassed by me. I guess everyone gets to that stage without even realising how it's happened. I'm not one of those loud parents that sings all over the street or smooches them audibly in front of their friends, but I guess kids can always find something about their parent that makes them cringe.

Chapter Three – Befriending Dogs

One day, I took my kids to the beach after school. It had been a bit of a trying week. It just felt like nothing was going our way and my mental health had taken a hit. I was ready for a blustery beach day to clear away the cobwebs. Thankfully, the storminess of the weather appeared to have put others off the same idea; we were close to being the only ones there. I'd brought a snack picnic, including hot chocolate to warm everybody up. After a play in the playground, we found a picnic bench to sit at. I dispensed the snacks, and everyone was sitting prettily, for a minute, anyway. They always are when there's a biscuit in their mouths. I couldn't even tell you what had gone wrong that week. Gladly, it's a distant memory now. It was probably a sum of small irritations that had got me in a bad mood. I just needed to rest and forget about it all. As I was sipping my hot chocolate, a dog approached us. Sometimes I'm in the mood for dogs – sometimes I'm not. It often depends on the owners and how much I want to talk to them. This one didn't have an owner in sight. That's always a warning sign, I think, but it was small and fluffy, so I didn't think much of it. It sniffed around us for a minute, I suppose, sussing out the snack situation. It was probably hopeful we'd drop it a crumb or two its way, or that we might be inattentive enough for it to snatch something from our hands. It was circling my legs and I was getting quite fond of it, despite my surly mood. Then, it did the dreaded thing – it lifted one leg in my direction. The dog peed on my leg. I guess it was aiming for the leg of the bench and something went wrong, but it didn't exactly feel like God was smiling down upon me in that moment.

The kids found it hilarious of course, and they proceeded to recount it to everyone we ran into in the days that followed. It has replaced the dog anecdote about the time my daughter had a biscuit stolen out of her mouth by a dog in the park. They thought that was traumatic; but my dog story was just hilarious. I have to admit, any time I think of it, I laugh. The funny thing is - it isn't the worst thing that has happened to us on a day out.

Mortified: A Motherhood Memoir

Chapter Four - Trying and Trying to go on Holiday

I thought I'd start small when it came to taking solo trips with my kids. We did go on a three-hour flight on two occasions – the first time was to my sister's wedding. The kids cried for the duration of the flight, and I was sure everyone on board was wishing bad things upon us – after the landing, of course. I could see that murderous rage in their eyes – the sleep-deprived airborne are not the most understanding of people. Travelling with two babies isn't something I'd recommend to anyone. I chain-smoked every minute I wasn't with my kids on that trip, after the landing of course. Still, with extra pairs of hands and the company of adults in the family, it was something that could just about be survived.

I decided a short road trip was enough to try on my own with two under threes. We've stayed in nearly every Airbnb in the country under the price of sixty pounds a night. One time, I decided to strike out and go further afield. We live in Belfast, and I decided to go to Enniskillen. I found the cutest little cottage online. It was tucked away from everything in the middle of the countryside. It sounded like bliss in the online description, and the photos didn't look half bad either. It even had a gypsy caravan in the front garden that we could also stay in if we wished. I knew it was a bit of a drive (anything is a bit of a drive with my kids, but this was an hour and a half, ie: an eternity.) We finally made it into the county, and we made a leisurely afternoon of it. We stopped at the castle and had a picnic. I found a playroom inside the museum that the kids adored. Everything was in our favour – then.

I looked up the directions to the house. I'm never exact about directions until I'm in the area. I aim for a general part of the country first, and if we manage that, then I'll get into the less important specifics, like where we're staying. A postcode had been provided by the host, but no directions. I supposed that the fact he hadn't provided more information was because the place was so remote. It must have been the only house with that postcode, and I assumed it would immediately become obvious when we were approaching it. It wasn't. We drove though the local village so many times I knew its only street like I knew my childhood village. Spar, post office, church, primary school, and back again – round and round we went. I should have asked for help at that point, but my pride got in the way. I wanted to make it on my own in the big, bad world. My family had always made fun of me, for how easily I got lost and I wanted to prove that I was someone that was good with directions. I wanted a good anecdote to take home from that trip – something much more positive than my usual stories. I had even contemplated not making use of Sat-Nav, but that would have been pure stupidity.

I drove in circles, mentally reassuring myself that I had to finally come across the property. With that little gypsy caravan on the front lawn – you couldn't miss it. I'd built it up so much to the girls that it had to happen; it couldn't become another disappointment. They were well used to my travel disasters by then. Finally, I pulled into a lane that led to somewhere concealed from the roadside. It had to be it; there was no other entry. I pulled in and immediately realised I'd made a mistake. The mud was thick on the ground, and it was swallowing my car tyres like quicksand. There wasn't room to turn around; even if I did a sixty-point turn, so I had no option but to keep going. I revved the engine, hoping it would get me through the worst of it. Having to be rescued from an unknown location was more than I could handle, and there was no longer any phone signal. The girls had noticed by then that we were in trouble, but I tried to laugh it off – telling them it was part of the adventure, even though the waterworks had started. Finally, I found a layby we could pull in to. It was a mission, but I got the car turned around and we got out of there. It practically needed to be power hosed after that. By the looks of the car, you'd have thought we'd spent years in the depths of the countryside, never thinking to give the car a wash. I was too stressed to worry about that though. I was just relieved to have got free from the swamp. I'd never find out where that lane led to, but I knew it couldn't be to our holiday home.

Conceding defeat, I drove back towards the all too familiar village. I decided to pull up at the Spar shop and go in to ask for directions. I knew I should have done that an hour earlier, but my pride had got in the way. At that moment, my phone battery died. Those were in the days before I thought to purchase essential items like phone chargers for the car. It just wasn't a consideration of mine. I was chiding myself for it then – that I'd spent my money on so many variations of the same dress, but I hadn't felt a charger was worth investing in. There was nothing I could do – I'd have to plough on without a functioning phone.

I pulled into a parking space and got the kids out of the car. I was sure I looked frazzled by then, and my hair was noticeably frizzier than usual. The girls could read the strain of it all on me, because they kept asking what was wrong with me and I couldn't bear to break it to them.

We went to the shop till, and the lady looked me up and down. She had a country lilt to her accent, and it just reminded me of how far we were from home.

"Sorry to bother you, but I'm lost, and my phone has died. Do you know where Hill Cottage is?"

I knew there couldn't be too many of them in the area; it was probably famous with the locals.

"Where?" she said, abruptly.

"Hill Cottage."

"What's that?"

"It's an Airbnb I booked but I can't find it.""

"Do you have the address?"

"The host just gave me the postcode."

"Did you contact him?"

"My phone died. You don't have a charger, do you?"

"No, we haven't got one here, sorry. Frank!" the lady shouted to a man standing behind me. He looked like a real farmer. His clothes were coated in mud, and he was wearing overalls that looked like they'd become like his second skin. His boots reminded me of thrillers when the camera pans down to the killer's shoes. They always look like that exact pair – the kind of wellies that make imprints like no other.

"Do you know Hill Cottage?"

"Aye, I know it. Is it a holiday place? John owns it, doesn't he?"

"Don't know – this lady is looking for it – can't find it."

13

It felt like the shop assistant was using as few words as she possibly could – like she couldn't be bothered wasting breath on me because I wasn't buying anything.

"Right – I'll tell you the directions," said Frank. "Have you got a pen?"

"No," I said. The lady at the till passed me a receipt to write on and a chewed biro. She gave me a look like I'd forgotten to put on clothes that morning. I felt just as naked as if I had.

The man proceeded to give me lengthy instructions on how to get to the cottage – none of which were in the direction I'd been looking. I frantically scribbled them down and thanked him, running back to the car. I had a feeling of peace then. I knew what I was about. The directions were so detailed I couldn't go wrong. I followed them and found the house he was talking about, but it didn't look familiar and there was no gypsy caravan out the front. I instantly knew it wasn't it. It didn't look anything like it had in the pictures and it was the only house in that area. I knew I was lost again, and I had to get back to civilisation before sunset. I turned the car around and headed in the direction of Enniskillen. I knew I'd never find that holiday house then. It would remain nothing but a nice notion – a holiday destination you never actually have the luck to make it to. I had to find somewhere to charge my phone. Then, I remembered I had a phone charger in my suitcase. I could have dug it out at the Spar and asked to make use of it, but I'd been spiralling so much then that I hadn't even thought of it.

Finally, we arrived in the town, and I felt relief wash over me. We needed to get dinner. We were all starving and I urgently needed to find a socket and a toilet. The kids were surprisingly patient. They took it all in their stride, like it was all a daily occurrence. Maybe in our family, that wasn't too far from the truth.

I walked into a colourful Mexican restaurant. It stood out with its friendly colours, and I hoped we might find some hospitality there. Plus, I really wanted a burrito. As soon as we walked in, I knew I'd made the right choice. The staff were actually from Mexico – it wasn't one of those Northern Irish Mexican eateries just posing as an authentic one. The aromas emanating from it were delicious and I liked that there was nothing pretentious about the place.

The staff smiled at me, and I contemplated falling into their arms and having a good cry, but I managed to control myself – just.

"Do you have somewhere that I could charge my phone?" I asked. "And a toilet?"

"Of course," the lady smiled. She looked at me like she could read the distress on my face. But maybe it would have been plain to anyone, however emotionally dense they might have been.

I felt like crying with joy. There's nothing quite like a disastrous holiday to make you appreciate your basic human needs. After taking everyone to the toilet, I ordered dinner: a burrito with mango salsa and beautiful turmeric rice. I got the girls the plainest burrito on offer to share between them. I knew they'd just deconstruct it to eat the bread, cheese and chicken anyway. They pulled it apart while I waited for my phone to charge. It was taking an eternity, but I was too hungry to mind. The girls were unwrapping their wrap, pulling the contents out all over the table, but I didn't have the energy left to get cross with them. It was the most amazing meal I remember eating, other than the toast with melted butter they give you after giving birth. It's always the meals you've worked hardest to earn or waited the longest for that you appreciate the most.

That was the end of that holiday. We headed home after that. I hadn't expected our return motorway trip to come so quickly but we were all relieved to be going home. I thought the girls might hold it against me. We had a conversation about it in the car and the fact that I'd disappointed them and that they hadn't got to have a holiday.

"It's OK, Mummy," they said, perfectly reasonably. "We still love you."

It was good to know that their love wasn't conditional, especially because I knew there would be other occasions when I'd need it not to be.

I hoped that would be our one and only trip with a ridiculous anecdote. But of course, it wasn't.

Chapter Five - Holiday in my Hometown

When the memory of that holiday had slightly faded, I decided to take my kids on holiday to the village I grew up in. It was a bit of a strange idea, especially considering the fact I'd spent my whole childhood dying to get out of the place. But the Airbnb sounded quaint, and it said there were chickens that came right up to the window. That sold me on it – I knew the kids would love it. We found it surprisingly easily, considering it was on a road I'd never even known was there. We pulled up in front of the cottage and I was instantly in love with the place. It was such a cute little old-Ireland style cottage. When we entered, the girls immediately went to the window seat that overlooked the clucking chickens. They came right up to the window, and they weren't a bit shy. They were obviously used to people being around.

The host had emailed me prior to our arrival to tell me the specifics I needed to know about the place. She said there was a garden we were welcome to use, so after we had unpacked, we went in search of it. There was a little gate adjacent to the property that led into the gardens. You couldn't see in from the outside, but that just added to the girls' curiosity about it. We entered and I closed the gate behind us. It felt like an old farm, and I didn't want to let any animals escape that might be roaming. I walked across the lawn, the girls skipping ahead of me. Then, they stopped abruptly.

"Keep going," I said, automatically. I'd said it on every walk we'd ever gone on. There is a lot of dilly dallying at their age. But they had stopped for good reason.

"Mummy," said one of my kids. "We need to run."

"Why?"

"The geese are coming to get us."

I squinted towards the horizon and saw a group of geese were marching purposefully towards us. I still didn't think anything would come of it. Maybe I just have little sense with regards to poultry.

"It's ok, just keep walking," I said. "They must live here."

"No, Mummy, let's go," said my daughter. She took my hand and started to pull me back towards the gate. At that point, the geese started to do that fly-walking thing they do when they're really worked up. The leader of the pack was particularly aggressive looking. They were gaining on us, and they looked ready to attack. I'd never known that I was scared of geese until that moment. It was like we were suddenly being hunted by feathered wolves.

"Run!" I yelled.

We all ran from the garden, screaming, and slammed the gate. The geese seemed determined to get us for trespassing on their property. I'd thought we were welcome to use the garden, but it was clear we were anything but. We went back into the cottage just to be on the safe side. I wasn't sure if they could fly, and I didn't want to chance it. Maybe the fact that we'd vacated their garden meant they didn't feel the need to hunt us down anymore.

I received an email shortly after that from the host, warning us not to set foot in the garden. The timing of its arrival made me wonder if she had seen the whole thing. She'd probably been laughing at us from her living room window. The email informed me there were geese there and that they were very territorial. She hadn't meant for us to make use of that particular garden. It was the only one we could see on the site, but when she'd said to make use of the garden in her email, it turned out she'd been referring to a walk along a country path that led to some distant land they owned. I guess I should have known that on some sort of psychic level.

The kids and I ventured out to the fields. It was quite a spooky walk. There wasn't a soul around and it was swampy underfoot. I got the sense that we could disappear from the face of the Earth, and no one would ever know. The trees were crooked, and they framed a beautiful early sunset. I pointed out the sunset to the kids, but they were busy worrying aloud about the creepiness of the surroundings and the potential for us to get lost. That had probably become a deeply engrained fear in them after the last holiday.

We walked along a stream and then doubled back on ourselves. We made it out of the wilderness, feeling both energised and relieved. I decided since darkness was rapidly closing in that it might be a good idea to stay inside for the night.

At night, the surroundings were a shade of black that only comes in the depths of the countryside with the absence of any streetlighting. Having lived in a city for years, it was hard to get used to it. The window with the seat at it didn't have curtains, and it was weird watching our own reflections in it, not being able to see what, if anything, was happening on the other side of the glass. I knew the chickens were probably in their hen house by then. Somehow, it would have comforted me a little, knowing they were still out pecking around out there.

I had an early night. After doing some writing at the kitchen table, and reading on the window seat, it felt fitting that I go to bed at a sensible hour. I didn't know what the following day held for us. But I was hopeful it wouldn't involve any angry birds.

We were woken at five in the morning by the rooster crowing outside. I liked the romance of that notion, in theory, but in reality, it made our start even earlier than usual. I've never been a morning person and when you get up that early in Winter, you can't even go outside to kill time because it's still dark.

We played about fifteen games of Go Fish and Uno. The kids squabbled in an even more enclosed space than usual. They got themselves dressed and picked at their toast, making more crumbs on the table and floor than I thought possible from uneaten toast. By the time I did the dishes and got myself ready, it was nearly seven AM. I was starting to regret having rented somewhere without a TV, thinking that a break from media would do us all some good. As it turned out, I didn't feel like bonding at 7AM. Thankfully, the girls had brought a stash of dolls and they started a game of their own down the side of the bed. I let them play until it turned into a fight, which never takes long.

Finally, when I could take no more, we went for a drive. I familiarised myself with the country roads and waited anxiously for the cafes and local National Trust property to open. 10AM had never felt so late in the day before. It turned out that one of the cafes in the village opened earlier than the others, but they only did takeaway coffee, so we ordered some overpriced coffee and hot chocolate and got it to go. The girls got s'mores hot chocolate. It sounded really special, but it was just hot chocolate topped with marshmallows and a name that meant 50p could be added to the total. We sat on a bench I've never seen anyone sit on before, in front of the church I was forced to go to as a kid that I'd hoped never to see again in my lifetime. The bench was right in the middle of the main street, so everyone was passing us on foot and by car. I prayed I wouldn't be spotted by anyone I knew. I hoped the earliness of the hour on a Saturday ensured that wouldn't happen. The girls drank a quarter of their hot chocolate and then asked to throw the rest away. I told them off for climbing on the bench about five thousand times. We were passed by some nosy elderly folk that felt the need to comment on our occupancy of the bench. There was a plaque on it in memory of someone. It somehow felt like we were sitting on their grave. That was probably what the passers-by thought anyway. It's the kind of town where that generation all know each other. They don't just know each other by name or sight; they know everything there is to know about each other. I was quickly remembering what had motivated me to leave in the first place.

I picked up some picnic food from the shop and we drove to the nearby National Trust property for a walk. We were the first to arrive and the man at the kiosk commented on our early appearance. The girls still had boundless energy while I lagged behind them, calling to them to wait for me and not to run into people. They tore up the grassy hill and rolled down it multiple times. I decided to do the same. It was fun at the start, but my body seemed to fall harder with each roll. I didn't know if it was my age or the extra weight I'd acquired in adulthood, but it felt like every bone in my body was simultaneously breaking. The kids were laughing at me, and that was worth something, at least. Hearing that joyous laughter you hear when you delight your children with something unexpected is one of the best things about motherhood. That, and wine when they're in bed.

We spent about four hours walking around the grounds. The girls climbed on every tree and jumped on every rock. I was glad of the place, because I didn't know what on Earth we would have done with our day otherwise. The rain started about half an hour after our arrival. We had our waterproofs on, but nothing is waterproof enough to keep you dry in four hours in the rain. We sheltered under a tree to have our picnic. The kids climbed on the branches of the tree while they ate their sandwiches and I sat, eating and feeling sorry for myself, even though we were on holiday, and I should have been grateful for every precious memory we were in the process of making.

19

When the rain got too heavy for our umbrella of trees, we went into the café. They still weren't doing sit ins. They've always had a lazy kind of attitude to everything and Covid suited them because it gave them an excuse to barely open at all. Anyway, I had another latte. I didn't really want it, but it was something to do. Afterwards, we went for a drive in the countryside. I was out of ideas by 2.30pm, so we pulled into a lay-by and played Hangman and Knots and Crosses in my journal at the side of the road.

When we got back to the house, I was just mentally working out what I'd make for dinner when the Airbnb host contacted me. I hadn't seen her face yet, even though she claimed to live in the neighbouring house. She was perfectly friendly, but she didn't seem to be on the ball about anything. Maybe living in such a sleepy place had made her sleepy herself.

"The power company are doing some work nearby, so I was just letting you know there won't be any electricity today."

She was so blasé about it that it was like she was saying there would be no hot tub for the night in a better kitted out property. I thought it mustn't have been anything truly disruptive. It'd probably be so short that if you blinked, you'd miss it. Except it wasn't. It was an all-day affair. Darkness was rapidly descending on us, and we had no lamps and every candle in the place was nothing but a melted piece of wickless wax. Then we discovered the next problem. The water wasn't working. I got in touch with the owner right away. It was one thing sitting in the dark with no TV; not being able to flush the toilet or get a glass of water was another thing entirely – and we were paying for the privilege. Thankfully, I still had data on my phone; it was probably only working because I'd brought it myself and didn't' come with the property. Other than the clothes we had and a few perishables in the fridge, there wasn't much left that was useable. I contacted the owner again. We didn't have to meet face to face for me to form a character profile in my imagination. She was one of those sluggish types nothing bothers. She said she had four kids of her own, but they were probably the free range kind that looked after themselves. They probably roamed outside and brought themselves up. They probably weren't even enrolled in school. Not that I was trying to be judgemental or anything.

"Yes, that happens with the water. We have our own tank so once it's done, it's done," she said.

I was scanning for the word "sorry," but I couldn't find it anywhere. In the meantime, my kids were simultaneously asking to go to the toilet and to have a drink of water. I felt like a terrible parent, having to hold them off.

"What do you do when it runs out?" I asked the lady, incredulous.

"We just wait for the tank to refill again," she said, like it was just one of those things. tt

Maybe I was just a spoilt city dweller that didn't think about all the amenities we had at our fingertips, but I knew we had to go. I couldn't even fill a bucket with water to flush the toilet, so I was out of ideas. I packed our suitcase and we all got into the car and drove away.

The lady didn't seem the least perturbed by the ordeal. She did refund us the second night and she offered us a second stay at a discounted rate, but I decided against holidaying there again - tempting though it was.

Chapter Six - The Time We Got Stuck in the Snow

There was a weather warning, but I never took those seriously. Living in Northern Ireland means you can't, or you'd never set foot outside. The weather was usually wrong anyway. If a thunderstorm was predicted you got a glorious summer's day; if we were told to set off for the beach, hail would inevitably follow. It was January and there was supposed to be snow; a skiff probably, I thought. Usually when it really snowed, we were surprised by it. Anything announced in advance ended up being nothing more than a light dusting of icing sugar.

I set off to my sister's house and the sky was its normal tone of grey. The ground was dry and there was no sign of iciness underfoot. I stayed for a couple of hours and caught up with my sister. She lived about ten miles away from me and we usually saw each other once a week. Nothing had gone majorly wrong with our visits up until that point.

When I was thinking about leaving, I looked out the window and was greeted by a scene of white. There wasn't a patch of dry ground visible. Everything was coated in thick snow, including my car, which looked more like a snowmobile by then.

"I'd better go," I said, looking apprehensively at the rapidly changing view. There was a steep hill right outside my sister's housing development and I'd never been confident driving in her town anyway – snow or no snow. I packed the girls into the car, and she told me to drive safely. It took me a good ten minutes to get out of her cul-de-sac. I started to descend the hill. I was only going about fifteen miles an hour, but I wasn't equipped to drive in those weather conditions. Suddenly, I felt myself losing control of the car. I did the one thing you're told not to do in snow: I braked, suddenly and violently. The car proceeded to slide down the hill; it spun, and I could see us rapidly approaching a car stopped ahead of us. I had a moment of relief when I realised the spin had caused us to miss the car, but then the back end of my car smashed into the rear end of hers. The kids were crying, and I felt like I'd left my body for a minute. I couldn't stop crying and

I didn't know what to do. I felt powerless and I was scared to move the car an inch in case I just worsened the situation. I could have been sitting there for five minutes or for twenty; I lost all concept of time. Finally, I snapped out of it enough to get out of the car. I knew there was someone waiting in the other car, but they hadn't come over in a fit of rage like I expected. The person was waiting, calmly, next to her car. It was an older lady with a kind face.

"I'm so sorry," I said. "I'm really, really sorry." It was all I was able to say. I made note of her phone number and registration and assured her I would contact my insurance company and let them know it wasn't her fault.

"Just get home," she said, softly. "You have kids in the car."

I was so grateful to her for not making a scene and for not adding to the stress of the event. She could have got angry, but she probably knew the weather was unusual. Since the accident, I'd noticed that several other cars were completely stuck in the snow on the same hill, and it wasn't because we were blocking the road. Several people were dealing with their own stressful situations all in the one spot. I climbed back into the car and phoned my sister. I told her I was going to try to come back to hers. Then, I turned the engine on. The car was refusing to ascend the hill. The road was both slushy and slippery and it was creating impossible driving conditions. After revving the engine for a while, I was just about to give up and I was considering getting a taxi home and leaving my car there, just so I could cry in the privacy of my own home, when an American guy approached my window. I wound it down.

"Can I give you a push?" he said. It felt like an angel had just shown up. There was something luminescent about him and it made it feel like it was a spiritual experience. Maybe I was just so stressed that I was having some sort of psychotic break.

The angel and his girlfriend pushed me up the hill. I tried to help with some revs, but they basically pushed me to the top of the hill with their bare hands. I thanked them profusely, but nothing could repay them for their kindness. I got back to the entrance to my sister's development and then I got stuck again. At that point, I panicked and phoned for recovery. I couldn't face another moment of crisis. They told me they'd send help, but in the meantime, I managed to get the car turned around and decided to head for home instead, so I told them not to worry. I went uphill instead, even though I had no idea how to get home that way. I made it much further and then got stuck at a roundabout. A man came to the window of the car. He tried to talk me through driving out of the snow. I didn't even know I was meant to start in second gear and keep the revs down. I think he saw my incompetence because he offered to get into the driver's seat for me. I let him. He got the car moving again and then gave it back to me. I was at the point that I gladly would have crawled home with my kids on my back. I didn't even know where I was, but I just kept going, as slowly as I could. The roads were complete chaos. Even skilled drivers were struggling. When I got to the motorway, I felt relief wash over me. That was when I knew I was likely getting home that day. The snow had melted away from the volume of traffic and it felt like I'd reached civilisation again.

The kids showed eternal patience that day, and I was so grateful to them for it. Their response to everything that happened inspired me to keep going. Sometimes when you have kids, you end up playing the role of the child and they become the adults. It's rare, but in those moments, you realise the reciprocal nature of your relationship. You don't just teach them; they teach you more than you ever thought you could learn from someone that mightn't even count in double digits yet.

Once I got home, everything went more smoothly. I got the car fixed and there was no fuss from the other driver or from the insurance company. That time was a particularly stressful period of my life in general, and at the time, I wondered why on Earth that had to happen on top of everything else. Now I realise that even though I didn't need the stress, I needed my faith restored in humanity. Strangers carried me home that day and the kind words of my kids kept me going. Sometimes you need something bad to happen to remind you of your precarious place on the Earth and to get you to accept help from others. Mums aren't always good at that. It feels unnatural to release the reigns on your life, but when you do, sometimes you're pleasantly surprised.

Chapter Seven - Having a House like in a Home Magazine

I remember when I moved into my first house with both of my kids, solo. It was a new build and I had visions of how it would look. I'd been waiting to have somewhere of my own to decorate as I pleased (even though I didn't own it.) By decorate, I mean adding knick-knacks and a couple of throws. I wasn't capable of anything beyond that anyway. The first sofa I ordered was completely impractical. It looked nice in the picture though, and it fitted in with my desired 1960's aesthetic. I still have it, and I still don't sit on it.

I can clearly remember the day it came. I was so excited. The people from the shop unpacked it, which was good because I didn't even know how to attach the legs. They unwrapped it from its cellophane wrapper. That was the first mistake. I should have asked them to keep it on, and then continued to keep it on for the next six years.

It was a lovely shade of yellow – the shade that kids always colour the sun in their preschool pictures. But it wouldn't stay that colour for long. As soon as the delivery guys left, I felt immediate regret sinking in. I'd spent six hundred pounds on getting the perfect sofa and it was too uncomfortable to sit on. I realised I wanted one of the ugly ones you could sink into and become one with when the kids were in bed. (Because that would be the only opportunity my bum would get to touch it.) The thing had a slanted back that worked against supporting a human back. You had to sit at a peculiar angle, and it was impossible to relax on it. It was like waiting on a train station bench – one of the metal ones that hurts like hell if you're there for longer than a minute.

The kids had it dismantled as soon as we got up the next morning. There were two cushions that were meant to stay on it, but they were obsessed with taking them off. It was a great game to them – like they'd walked into a free soft play centre. It's been a rough life for that sofa, but not as much as for my other one. We got a second sofa shortly after that – as soon as I could justify the purchase. I got tired of sitting on a bench while I read and watched TV. So, we got a cord monstrosity with two inbuilt recliners and cushions that felt like clouds if they had substance. It's been well-used and well-loved and covered in the crumbs of every pizza and snack we've had on it. It also has stuffing hanging out at the top of it because my kids have used it as a trampoline and climbing wall for so many years. I won't replace it though – however ripped it gets. I've told myself I'm not buying new furniture until they're at least eighteen.

The furniture is one thing. It's going to get worn, even when handled relatively delicately (which it isn't, obviously.) But it's much more maddening when other parts of your house are dismantled and defaced for no good reason. Some things are just sitting there, like temptation waiting for your kids' imaginations to latch onto. My kids have colourful imaginations of their own – especially when it comes to creative forms of destruction.

One time, I was sitting, in what I thought was well-earned peace in the living room at night. The kids had slept remarkably well for the last hour. Usually there were constant stirrings and crying to alert me to the fact they didn't want to be in bed, needed a drink, needed me to wheel out a portable mini bar filled with whatever treats they desired. There had been deathly silence. It almost made me uneasy. Then I heard a rustling, and my suspicions were confirmed. I went upstairs. Both ends of the stairs were protected by stair gates. I didn't know if the safety element outweighed the impracticality of them and the fact that they so often slowed me down when I needed to run up or down – usually in response to a demand that could have waited a few seconds longer.

On this occasion, I got to the top of the stairs, and I knew the noise was coming from my room rather than from my daughter's. She was seated in the middle of my bed with my make-up bag emptied all over the duvet. She was smearing make-up all over her face. It was cute that she was mimicking me, but in that moment, that observation evaded me. I just saw the crazy mess on my bed. It was like one of those film moments when a canine has been brought into the family home and the climactic moment arrives when they consider rehoming it because it has destroyed all their possessions. My duvet cover was destroyed – the new one that had perfectly matched the rest of the accessories in the room. My cushions were covered in a foundation paste. I knew by looking at them that there was no way it was going to come out in the wash. The once-cute owl was destroyed, and it didn't have visible facial features left. I cleaned all the make-up off my one-year-old, which she wasn't a bit happy about. I had to throw out one of my make-up cloths because she had such a heavy coating of blusher on her face. It wasn't confined to the cheekbones. It had been spread across the entirety of her face and it was hard to get it off without scrubbing her perfect skin. It felt like my baby had somehow spoiled herself, and for a moment, I saw how grotesque the idea of make-up could be – until the following morning when I reapplied mine, anyway. It was a lifeline of sorts – something that prepared me to face my day. I made sure after that that my make-up bag was stored on top of the bathroom cabinet. It felt like there was nothing left at eye level anymore, and certainly not at ground level. It was easier to babyproof everything, even if I had to get onto a stool to reach every item I owned. Admittedly, that was a bit of a pain.

I thought the make-up incident was a one-off. I hoped it was. I've never been so wrong about something before. The bed being destroyed still stands out in my mind as a memorable incident, but not an isolated one.

The most pervasive problem has been the toothpaste. Since my daughter started brushing her own teeth, she has done everything possible to rid herself of the toothpaste, other than actually allowing it to touch her teeth. My least favourite place that she has scraped it onto is the underside of the radiator. It's not somewhere you would think to look for smears of toothpaste, even after it has been done once before. I just don't spend a lot of my life looking behind radiators to check for dirt. It always becomes apparent after some build-up has occurred – usually when I'm sitting on the toilet and in a hurry to leave the house. It starts dropping off onto the floor like chunks of chipped paint. Then I realise I need to attend to it, or it's going to become unconquerable.

I never would have guessed that dried toothpaste would be so hard to clean. The paint on my radiator has already worn away to reveal the rust beneath and the remaining rough surface had become one with the toothpaste. It's a miserable job. I always promise myself that my daughter will clean it herself next time, but she's always at school when I find it. She has one of those personalities, like someone who flees the scene of a crime before anyone has a hope of pinning it on them. Her dad and I aren't together. I tell myself that's a quality she inherited from him.

A few years ago, I found a 1960's footstool in an antique shop. I had actually managed to look around a place filled with breakables without major incident. Both of my kids were with me at the time, so that bordered on the miraculous. They got a pair of sunglasses each, in January, and I got my footstool. It was particularly unique because it doubled up as a small magazine rack. It had a leather cushion for the lid and there was something about it that vaguely reminded me of a storage box that my grandad kept in my mum's old bedroom – even though that one was purple and furry. Anyway, the point was – I was pleased to find it. A few months later, I opened the lid one day – something I never felt the need to do, since as far as I knew, there was nothing inside it. It was filled with sweets that had developed into fluffy mould. They were only recognisable as sweets because of the empty Haribo packet that identified them. The mould had become so glued to the wood that it had rotted the entire wooden inside of the footstool. I knew there was no point in even trying to clean it, so I said goodbye to it that day. Maybe that was the moment when I realised it was a waste of money investing in anything for the sake of home improvements. I'd have to save that until I reached retirement age.

When I mentioned the incident to my kids, they played dumb. They acted like they had no idea how the sweets might have got there; in fact, they denied any awareness of the presence of a footstool in our house, in general. I didn't know which was worse – the act of destruction, or the string of lies. I thought they'd stop there; I thought - how many times can kids cope with disappointing their parents and continue in the same vein? I was wrong again.

When the girls still shared a double pram, I used to spend hours walking around the town we lived in at the time: Bangor. It has recently been named a city. I don't know how it achieved that status because nearly every building there was boarded up by the time we left. I always thought cities had shops in them, and amenities, but maybe I was wrong. One of the things I did love about Bangor were the treasures I found in charity shops there. I don't know why I did, because it seemed to be a seaside spot, mostly for the over sixties that wanted a place of sanctuary after a lifetime of slaving away and climbing the social ladder, waiting for their first opportunity to jump off it.

One day, I spotted the perfect doll's house in the window of one of the shops. It looked unused, but it was an old-fashioned dolls' house with a charm you can't buy first hand. I knew the girls would love it. Maybe on some level, I thought I would love it too. It was the kind of the toy I knew I would have adored as a kid. I used to have a Sylvanian Families house. I'll never forget the time we had a playdate with a boy that lived on our street. He broke one of the legs off the coffee table and I was devastated. I held a grudge too - because I never liked him after that. To be honest, I hadn't been crazy about him to begin with. But I couldn't stand rough children that didn't look after things. That's what makes it so ironic I've ended up with two of my own. I try to instil the idea in them that they should value their possessions and the possessions of others and treat them with respect. It doesn't work. They just don't seem to care.

About a month after I bought that beautiful dolls' house, they ripped the window boxes and the frames off the outside of the house. I put it down to their age and thought they'd treat it with more care as they got older. At the age of six and seven, I was looking at the house, realising how much it had changed in a small number of years. There are toys in my mum's house, that she produces at intervals – some from the 1960's when she was a child that are still in much better condition than that house was. The roof had been bent back to the point it had snapped off and there were pieces of wood that jutted out like shards of glass. It had probably become a bit of a safety hazard, so I ended up removing the roof covering altogether.

One day, I was cleaning while my kids were at school. I had the time to do more than the usual surface clean, so I actually opened the doors of the dolls' house. I was shocked by what I found. It was impossible at first glance to work out what it was; it looked like a scene from a house of horrors. On closer inspection, I worked out that there were hundreds of pieces of decayed fruit lying all over the floors of the house. I didn't know how it had gone unnoticed for so long. I hadn't even smelt anything suspect. When the girls got home from school, I gave them a stern warning and I said if it ever happened again, I'd dispose of the house. I'd had to spend a good portion of my afternoon scrubbing the house. It was one of the most disgusting things I've ever had to do. I gladly would have dealt with a runny nappy over that. I hoped never to have to relive it.

A few months later, I happened to open the dolls' house to return a stray sofa to the living room in it. I found the same scene again. It was beyond belief. It was much worse than the previous time. The floor had rotted beneath the fruit. The entire house was destroyed. I didn't even attempt to clean it up. I just packed it up into the car to drive to the dump. I hoped it would be a lesson that would stay with my kids, and they'd never repeat it again.

When I asked them about their reasoning behind the disgusting creation, they said it was because they didn't want the fruit I gave them as snacks, so they had just hidden it in the house. I don't know why kids think if you hide something it will vanish for ever and no one will ever uncover the evidence or have to deal with it.

They have been creative in their forms of destruction. They come up with ideas I never would have dreamt up in a million years of boredom. If only they would use those ideas for good. Once, I had some dry shampoo sitting in the bathroom. The girls went and got it and sprayed it all over the logs in the fireplace. It's a good job they are just there for show because it could have caused an explosion had it been lit. Some things, I assume, are common sense – you just don't do the things. But my kids like to learn through experimentation – usually with things with a real element of danger to them. They like to hoard sweet wrappers in places they think I'll never look, but there is always a giveaway – a piece of coloured paper peeking out, a funky smell, a trail of crumbs. They used the front opening of the fire grating as a storage space for unpermitted sweet wrappings for a while. It never ceases to amaze me how often they sneak things, knowing I won't be happy, and that I will find out each time. Mums always find out. Maybe not at the first available opportunity, but it always comes out in the end, unlike some of the stains they have made on my décor.

My sister and I often swap stories on the unbelievable behaviours of our children. It must be a genetic problem. I always seem to meet people that have peaceful kids that are compliant and always appear to do what they're told – at least in public. I think those parents congratulate themselves on their parenting techniques when it actually just comes down to luck and personality. Being strong-willed and a person that is never daunted by things may serve them well in later life, but it doesn't serve the parents well in early life. I can't imagine asking my kids to do something and having them agree to it straight away, or not doing the exact opposite, for that matter.

I often wonder if I should take a different tack and start telling my kids to do the opposite to what I want them to do. For example: "throw yourself on the road," might make them show particular caution when crossing one. Or "keep touching that very breakable ornament" might make them treat it with some care.

I'll never forget the time my kids went for a sleepover at my sister's house. It was before she'd had her own kids and she probably had visions of the slow-paced days we used to spend with my grandmother in our own childhoods. We were particularly compliant children, and she still told us off, but my kids are a different breed entirely. I believe my sister picked the girls up – that part hasn't stayed with me. It's been overwritten by what came next. I waited, anxiously, for her to text me to come and pick them up early. It felt like a huge undertaking – having them overnight. There's a bit of a difference between seeing kids for a couple of hours with family and having them to yourself for twenty-four hours. I knew they wouldn't sleep. I prayed they would, but I knew they wouldn't. It was strange having an afternoon to myself. Even though I'd dreamt about it for so long, it was hard to know what to do. I felt empty handed, walking around without my kids and all their belongings. I was used to having a pram, a buggy board, and a nappy bag everywhere I went. It was odd, being able to carry a small handbag with me and to fit everything inside. I felt like I'd forgotten everything I'd programmed myself to remember.

At first, it appeared that there was no visible reason to sound the alarm. I asked how things were going by text and I got an "ok," from my sister. She's never been talkative by text, so it wasn't necessarily a sign of anything bad, but I was imagining fifty scenarios in my head – none of them good. My sister had always been someone that suffers in silence too, so I was aware that she might completely hide any of my kids' wrongdoings from me. I just hoped they would sleep. I knew they'd be hard work while they were awake – that was a given. But at least if they slept, it'd be manageable.

I agreed to meet my sister and her husband with the kids at my parents' house the following day since we were all going there for dinner. When I got out of the car, I saw the same strained expressions on their faces that I was used to wearing myself. It was that weary look – the one that said – I've had to tell someone off five times a minute since yesterday, and on little to no sleep.

The kids gave me an enthusiastic hello and then ran off to whatever they had started at my mum's house – probably Playmobile or something involving the iPad (my daughter still calls my dad's iPad "the love of my life.")

"What happened?" I asked my sister. Her husband interjected. "They broke a family heirloom."

"What?"

"They were supposed to be in bed – they'd been told to get in bed and stay in it a few times."

I knew he was downplaying that part. It was probably closer to ten dozen, going by what they did on the average night at home.

"You know the deer ornament that Grandma left us when she died?" asked my sister.

I immediately pictured the exact fawn like I'd seen it earlier that day. Why do images from childhood remain that crystal clear? It felt like I was struggling to remember the spelling of my own name at that point, but I remembered the figurine from twenty years ago. I wondered if my own kids would remember it beyond that day. I doubted it.

"Yeah, what happened?"

"They were climbing up and lifting stuff off the bookcase and it got dropped."

"Oh, no. Did it shatter?"

"No, the ears broke off it, but we've superglued them back on. It's drying at the moment, so we don't know what it'll be like."

I thought about offering to buy another one, but I knew that was a ridiculous proposition. They'd probably been mass produced in the 60's and it was the only remaining one that had been intact – prior to its encounter with my kids, anyway.

I scolded them, but they didn't seem to understand what they'd done wrong. That was becoming a bit of a theme. They were playful kids that didn't value many physical objects – other than a couple of teddies and some threadbare blankets. They were breaking my stuff all the time, so I was well used to it, but I knew it would be a shock to a couple that didn't have kids yet.

As I reminisce about the "good" times, I remember a time when my kids were toddlers. I had gone for a quick shower. At the time, we were living in a small flat with everything on one floor. The kids toddled in and out of the bathroom while I raced through my shower. The place was baby proofed to the extreme. There wasn't an item within reach that I thought they could get. But I didn't give them credit for their creative endeavours. I had a clock that I'd bought prior to having kids. It had travelled around with me too. I'd had it adorning my bookcase in Glasgow when I'd lived there. It was a sturdy thing that had survived being bumped around in my suitcase a good few times – only wrapped in clothing for a little protection. It was a carved wooden beauty, painted white, with two legs and a traditional clock face. It was something I thought I'd always keep. It was just one of those ageless items that goes with everything.

In the short time I'd been occupied with washing myself, my kids had somehow managed to pry the glass cover off the clockface. I hadn't even known it was possible to do such a thing without tools, a workshop and great skill. It seemed like one of those things that was reserved for experts and even then, only when there was a major fault to attend to. The glass cover was lying on the floor, and they had pulled both hands off the clock. I looked at the sad-looking time-teller lying on the floor. I knew it was destined for the bin. I didn't have the energy to contemplate fixing it, and it was pointless, with kids as curious as mine. It felt like everything I treasured needed to be strapped to the ceiling if I wanted it to last longer than five minutes. I had practically already done that with all my toiletries, cleaning products and sharp objects, but I hadn't realised my clock was in danger. I got over it quickly, but the memory still pops into my mind now and again and I shake my head in disbelief. At least that one was easier to clean up after than the dolls' house. But after that, I was a little more hesitant each time I entered the bathroom for any longer than a minute.

Chapter Eight - The Circus – The Literal Kind

I am always googling activities to do with my kids. It's partly out of the desire to spend quality time and make lasting memories with them, partly out of sheer desperation to get out of the house and get them unglued from my legs. The second reason might slightly outweigh the first. I love finding free events. It's not that I'm a complete cheapskate, but I never have a lot of money, so it's one of the only options. Maybe if I could keep my clicking fingers off clothing websites, we'd have a little more, but we aren't one of those families that can afford to go to a paying attraction every day of the week, especially in the current climate.

On one of those days, I was delighted to see that there was a "Festival of Fools" on in Belfast for a few days. My boyfriend does breakdance and acrobatic tricks, so I knew it would interest him too. I just never thought I'd be the featured fool for the day. The guide was vague about what exactly the event entailed, but it looked kid-friendly, so I was in. We got to Writer's Square in the Cathedral Quarter, and we were some of the first people to arrive. Usually, I'm always in the back row at those things, but for once, we weren't. We even got to use the little foam cushions they were passing out with the event name printed on them. That felt like a special privilege. Cold and numb bums on concrete were just part of the experience though. The first show we saw was a clown performance with tapes used as a prop in each part of their act. They used it to mark out boxes on the ground to perform acrobatics in, they juggled the rolls of it and tied each other up with it. I wasn't overly interested in it, but it was something to do with the kids, and they seemed mildly interested in it. When it ended, the event workers moved us along to the next spot. We were right in the front row for this one. We weren't sure what it was; there was just a funny looking little house at it with ropes hanging from the top and a reference to crows on it. We sat for a while and there was no sign of life, even though a crowd was building. I'd thought at first that we were one family of ten, but suddenly, there were hundreds of people there.

The show started with a crow puppet appearing from the upstairs window, Punch and Judy style. I thought that was the entirety of the show – a dancing, mischievous crow on a stick, but there were clowns involved too. They just didn't look like the conventional ones. They didn't have the red noses, but they had the brazenness that's characteristic of all clowns I've met. The first to appear stuck her bum out from behind the house and wiggled it at the crowd to get the show started. Then, she performed a silly skit and the crowd warmed up to her. There were three ladies in the show. The work that had gone into it was impressive and they worked hard to involve the crow. It was like the pantomime for kids in the Opera House, I thought – funny but not stressful. There's a line that can quickly be crossed, as I was soon to find out.

A man I would place in his sixth decade was seated front centre in the crowd. I thought he must have quickly regretted his seating choice. He was singled out multiple times. He had his grandchildren with him, and they were probably loving every minute of it. He didn't look like someone that would naturally want to be involved at all. Maybe that was why he was recruited. I guess it looks funnier if the person looks out of their element. Everyone was laughing hysterically at their antics – myself included. But I simultaneously felt so sorry for the man that had been dragged into the show – probably against his will. Each time one of the clowns entered the audience, I froze. I don't often pray now, but I did send one out into the ether that day. I prayed they wouldn't pick me. They hadn't pulled anyone onto the stage yet. They were just torturing them in the relative safety of the audience. One of the ladies in the show feigned sadness in response to one of her fellow actors and jumped onto the sixty-something man's knee. He cradled her like a baby – it was all forced; he had no say in it. I wondered if his wife minded. She wasn't laughing as heartily as everyone else. It felt like a boundary had been crossed, but as my boyfriend said later that day – that's what circus performances are all about. If you don't want to be involved, you shouldn't go. That was the grave error I made.

There was a baby doll in the show, and they played a tape of a baby crying inconsolably. They dragged the same gentleman up to the front, dressed him up in a bonnet and apron, forced an oversized baby bottle into his hand and told him he was the baby's nurse. He was given a seat, so he had to stay there, feeding and rocking the baby. He looked very uncomfortable, but he handled it well and with grace. He smiled and played along. I wondered how I would fare in a similar situation. Little did I know, my opportunity was rapidly approaching.

At one stage, a performer had forced her way through the audience, pressing mine and my daughter's heads to the sides to get through. I hoped that would be the extent of our engagement. Of course, I was wrong. There was a scene where they needed a policewoman. Before I could grasp what was going on, I had a hat shoved on my head and my arms were forced into an oversized black jacket. The lady announced to the audience that I was the most intimidating police officer she had ever seen, and everyone laughed. With my blonde curls and shy manner, I guess that was why they picked me out. I get that contrast is funny, but I don't want to be involved the delivery of the comedy; I'd rather watch and appreciate it from the side lines. I get ridiculously easily embarrassed, and I get embarrassed for other people too, so it was a perfect nightmare for me, but I knew I had to play along. I did what they told me to do – just at a lesser level than they wanted from me. I didn't pound the door like they told me to; I knocked it. I didn't holler; I spoke at my usual level. I tried to run away at one point and the lady dug her nails into my arm. "Don't dare try to run away again," she growled at me. So, I did as I was told. The whole ordeal dragged on interminably. I wished I would have the good fortune to collapse so someone could call an ambulance and get me out of there. I was having palpitations and my anxiety was through the roof. Had someone asked me to pen my worst imaginable experience, that would have been it.

I thought, at the very least, that I'd make a quick escape, but I was involved in a never-ending scene. The lowest points were whenever they fed me grapes with their bare feet, forced a cake in my mouth and spilt a cup of tea in my knee. Thankfully it was cold. I laughed it all off, but they knew I was hating every moment of it. I thought the audience could feel it too. It was filled with strangers - with the exception of one family I knew from the school run, and I'd probably never see them again, but I was still mortified. Having kids seems to invite so many situations you never would have put yourself into otherwise.

I finally got my opportunity to run away. A man was pulled up from the audience and forced to stand in a bridge position on the tabletop. The ladies proceeded to stack themselves on top of him in a human pyramid. I was wondering how they got away with it all in the trepidatious territory of 2022. You weren't allowed to look at someone the wrong way or they could sue you. So, how had they evaded the legal system that supposedly protected citizens from food allergy exposure, injury and mental suffering? I knew I was thinking too seriously about the whole thing, but it took me at least a week to come down from the heightened anxiety caused by it all. Maybe I was just grumpy because I'd gone for too many years without sleep. Motherhood has definitely lowered my tolerance for silliness. I can only deal with so much before I turn into something closely resembling a rabid dog.

After the show, I vowed never to sit in the front row at an event again. The embarrassment of it all would haunt me for weeks to come. It was increased by the fact a teacher from my daughter's school approached me the following Monday morning at drop-off. "I recognise you," she shouted. "You're the lady from the circus at the weekend, aren't you?"

I nodded reluctantly, wishing I didn't have such recognisable hair and that it was possible to deny the whole thing. "My daughter asked me if they asked the participants to join in before the show, or if they got volunteers. But I said to her, "I don't think that lady knew she was going up there.""

"Yeah, it was my version of hell," I said, laughing it off.

"You did look really uncomfortable," she said, laughing. "Bye."

My fear was confirmed: it was obvious I had hated every moment of it. After the show, my kids told me it was funny having me up there. I guess at least someone enjoyed it.

"Wasn't it obvious I didn't want to be there?" I asked my daughter.

"Yes, from your face," she said, simply.

Sometimes I wish I had a face that hid what I was thinking a bit better.

Chapter Nine – Pampered in Hospital

It's weird the way you can sense danger as a mum, even when you initially think you're over-reacting. One day, I went to a friend's house with my kids. We had another friend that was meeting us there with her kids too. There were a lot of us in the house and it was an expansive house. It used to be a guest house and every room had an ensuite and a fire door. The kids loved it, of course. It probably felt like a sprawling mansion to them. There were one baby and six kids in the building. They all got insanely hyper when they saw each other. They would run wildly around the house, squealing like we used to on the fortuitous occasion when the ice-cream van drove round. Now kids have an ice-cream in their mouths every five minutes and it's nothing special anymore.

The three of us (the mums) always took the opportunity to sit down, drink coffee, chat, wash dishes and dispense snacks. The kids ran in every few minutes, so we knew they were all ok. But I always had a bad feeling in my gut – like there was an accident waiting to happen. It all just felt too mad in that house. They were like feral animals when they got together, all of them equally strong-willed and dynamic.

The day finally arrived – the one I'd pessimistically always known about in the pit of my stomach. We were sitting talking and taking the first sip of our well-deserved coffees when a gut-wrenching scream came from the hallway. I got to my feet and rushed out. I couldn't even recognise the child's voice because the screams were so piercing. I can still hear them now. It was my younger daughter, and she was clutching her hand, but I couldn't make sense of anything she was screaming. My other daughter enlightened me as to what had happened.

"Her hand got closed in a door."

My heart sank. It was always a horrible injury to get as a kid. I could remember closing my own hand in a door at home and how painful it had been, but the doors in that house were particularly heavy. They swung shut on their own.

I'd never seen my child so hysterical before. It was heart-breaking to watch and there was so much blood. I carried her into the bathroom and tried to figure out how to stop the bleeding. I bundled her hand in a wad of tissue and my friend brought me a plaster. It was kind of her, but I knew it was more serious than that. I just had that instinctive feeling a mum gets about their own child. I rushed out of the house with my other daughter without a goodbye and drove straight to the hospital. My daughter got an X-Ray that revealed her finger was broken; not just that – she'd have to have surgery too. The nail bed was so badly damaged they had to repair it, or it wouldn't heal properly.

It was a lot of information to take in. I felt sick with worry. I don't know how parents of seriously sick children cope with the news. They must be much stronger people than me. Once my daughter knew what was happening, she was OK. She didn't seem to be in pain anymore and she was enjoying being fussed over. We were moved to a children's ward, and she was put in a bed. She loved the fact it was adjustable. She pushed the button that levered her headrest up and down constantly. A nurse got us settled and brought some toast and a jug of juice for her. She was loving that – it was at the stage when I was still stingy with sugar, and she had an entire pitcher of diluted blackcurrant to herself. She was chugging it like she was involved in an adults' drinking game. My other daughter almost seemed like she was getting jealous of the attention and the special privileges that came along with breaking a bone. The injured daughter made a big deal of her toast. You would have thought it was a platter of Haribo, the way she was talking about it. She was good at making her sister jealous and starting a fight, even when she was wounded.

I'd been told by the hospital that my other daughter couldn't stay with us. It was very understanding of them, considering I was a single parent, and I didn't have family living nearby. (Note: sarcasm.) I was given instructions to have her removed from the hospital and passed on to a family member. I hoped there would be a contactable and willing relative. I knew she was probably feeling a bit pushed out of the nest after the ordeal, but she was worried about her sister too – even though the same sister that had been in audible pain an hour earlier was now happily chattering away and asking me to change her DVD every five minutes. She was almost obnoxiously happy to be a hospital patient. I felt wearied by the whole experience. It was only one o'clock in the afternoon and I felt like I was ready for bed. I didn't know when I would see my bed – I didn't know how long the whole thing would take. Thankfully, my mum was able to take my other daughter. I guess if she couldn't, they would have just put her out onto the streets to fend for herself. That's the health service in Northern Ireland for you.

I stayed at my daughter's bedside, worrying about her operation. I didn't know how parents coped with major surgery. Just having her put to sleep filled me with fear. She didn't know about the details; I just told her she'd be going for a wee nap, that her nail would be fixed, and she'd see me as soon as she woke up again. She didn't seem perturbed by that. She just watched Scooby Doo and Peppa Pig back-to-back and drank most of her pitcher of juice until she wasn't allowed to anymore. We had to make countless trips to the toilet, which I found out was an undertaking with one of her hands resembling a club. She was enjoying having her arm bandaged up and swinging it around like a baseball bat. I guess kids like attention, no matter what form it comes in. I, on the other hand, would have much preferred to have been spared the whole catastrophe.

I waited for her to go into the operating theatre. We were told she wasn't a priority, so any emergencies would go in front of her, but equally, if there were cancellations, they might move it forward. I just wanted it to be over. I sat in the bedside chair, serving snacks and neglecting all my own basic needs. I hadn't had a drink of water since entering the ward hours earlier, but if you weren't a patient, nobody cared. I wondered why they didn't at least have a vending machine for the parents, or a coffee station, or something. It was a different visit than my last one there – when I had given birth to my daughter. She was three, and it felt like we'd done quite well to stay away for that long. Most parents I knew had been in and out of A&E after various park and trampoline incidents. I'd never liked trampolines and I tried to minimise the number of times the girls went on one. I was even more wary of them after a friend told me her mother-in-law was bouncing on one at the start of a birthday party once and ended up breaking her back and being rushed to hospital. They were death traps, as far as I was concerned. But we still hadn't escaped A&E. It felt like a rite of passage for all parents of young children. I remembered back to the time I'd been there myself with a broken wrist and I'd had to undergo surgery too. I was about ten at the time, and I felt like an inept parent, thinking that my daughter was only three years old when she had to go through the same thing. There's nothing like walking into hospital with your kid to humble you as a parent – not that I'd ever possessed any real confidence thanks to professionals that are paid to put you down from day one (ie, health visitors.)

In the late afternoon, I was told that my daughter was going to the theatre. I wished we were going to a different kind of show. She was excited to be taken through the corridors on a bed with wheels. I was smiling as much as my face could muster, trying to be brave for her. She has always been brave and bull-headed, so she probably didn't need any reassurance. She was chatting to all the hospital staff like they were cherished employees of hers with whom she'd been working for the entirety of a lengthy career. She never ceased to surprise me with her boundless confidence. I wished I could pinch some of it for myself.

The nurse whispered to me that I could stay with her until she was asleep and then wait outside while they performed the surgery. I was grateful for that – that my face would be one of the last she'd see before her induced nap. I waited by her bedside until she started to count backwards with me, not making it to two. She looked so peaceful lying there; more peaceful than she had ever looked in her sleep before. Maybe the drugs helped with that.

I waited anxiously on a chair in the corridor. I was right in front of a set of automatic doors. They opened and closed constantly, bringing a chill with them each time. Various doctors and nurses passed me, laughing and chatting. It reassured me, that none of them looked flustered or distressed. I knew there were people in hospital for much more serious surgery than hers, but when it's your three-year-old, it feels like you've become very small and helpless in the vast world, like you're holding on for dear life by one single frayed thread.

The doctor came out of the operating theatre to reassure me that she was fine. He explained every part of the procedure to me. The fact that he was calling it a procedure helped. It made it sound routine and like it wasn't a big deal. At that point, he told me that on average, they had seven kids in a week with the same injury, same operation and the same bad luck with a door. I didn't feel so abnormal when he said that.

Her operation felt like an eternity, but finally, they told me she was beginning to stir and that it was time for me to return to the room. The nurse said I could climb into the bed with my daughter, and they'd wheel us back to the ward together. It was a special moment; the beautiful ones you'll never forget often come from turmoil and strife. Still, I hoped that would be our last hospital visit for the foreseeable future.

She still talks about the toast and how amazing it was watching Peppa Pig in bed all day. You'd think it was a luxury hotel the way she recounts the tale. Sometimes she even says she wishes she'd break something else so she can go back. It's weird how much kids are willing to endure for special attention and snacks in bed.

Chapter Ten – Pecked to the Post

One day, I took the girls for a seaside picnic. We were living near the seaside at the time, and I wanted to make full use of it. It was Summer, by name, but the weather wasn't in agreement with that at all. I brought a picnic blanket and a proper picnic, packed in our cool bag on the back of the pram. I didn't have a car then and if you added a feather to the handle of the pram, it tipped over. I'd found that out in the food court when the girls had been having a nap in the pram and a stranger had tapped me on the shoulder to tell me that the girls were lying with their feet in the air. Thankfully, they hadn't even noticed or woken up, but there's something incredibly shame-inducing about being informed of something you've failed to notice as a parent. I'd been too busy staring out the window at the swooping seagulls. It was rare that the girls were both asleep at the same time, so when they were, my brain immediately switched off and I sat in a daze. My Burger King coffee tasted like there was no caffeine in it, but I probably needed a quadruple shot then, just to feel reasonably human. Not much has changed in that respect, not even as my kids get older. They still never sleep through the night. They never have. At the ages of eight and almost seven, I had hoped they'd at least do it on occasion. Maybe I just wasn't mean enough when they got into my bed and now, they think it's a free for all. There is no corner of the house I can call my own - unless I banish them from the kitchen. Sometimes if I'm cooking and cleaning or writing in there, they know to steer clear because I probably seem peri-menopausal if they don't.

Anyway, that summed up a persistent problem I had with the pram. The balance was off, even when there was little weighing the handle down. Food shopping was a nightmare. I had a metal ring that bags clipped onto, but because the pram couldn't support the weight of them, I had to lift and wheel the pram at the same time. It was like taking an overfilled wheelbarrow everywhere with me. If anyone started crying in the midst of that, I felt like I was dying inside. I'd pass mums in their big seven-seater cars. Everything looked a breeze with a car like that. They could fit everything inside it. I just ended up carrying everything like a pack mule. When the time came for me to move into my new house, I bought a suitcase and carried it with one hand whilst pushing the double pram with the other. It felt like some sort of ridiculous parents' race – I had to carry as much as I possibly could without falling over and I seemed to always have a sore back. There are some days that rain down on you harder than others though – emotionally speaking. I remember the pram I had before that. It was just a one seat buggy I'd used for my older daughter when I was heavily pregnant with my second. I'd been about as far as I could get from where we were staying at the time when the wheel just inexplicably fell off the pram. I had to carry my daughter home and abandon the broken pram at the side of the road. Fly-tipping might be illegal, but sometimes there's good reason for it – like when you're about to give birth and your only form of transportation for your other child breaks down on you. I never hear stories like this from other people; I don't know if they're just private about their misfortunes or if I'm just an accident-prone type of person.

Back to where I started this chapter - the picnic that I'd had in mind didn't exactly go to plan. I found a quiet patch of grass next to the playground. We were the only ones there. Usually when you go for a picnic, everyone and their granny is there; when they're not it's usually a sign of something you don't know about that everyone else does. I don't know how they always get such insider information. Maybe they regularly use the weather app on their phones. I gave up on mine long ago because it always gave me the wrong predictions. There was a stormy sky when we got all our picnic items spread out on the blanket. The threat of rain cast itself over us, but it didn't come. Maybe I had just picked a moment when all other mums were in work. I seemed to be one of the only stay-at-home mums in my generation. My announcement of that title always drew disapproval from strangers. But maybe, on reflection, they were wiser to stay in their offices.

We started eating. The kids were at that stage where you have to promise them all your worldly possessions to persuade them to take a bite of their sandwich. Unless, of course, they decided to play with their food instead. Then they'd sit for a long time, making a mess and not eating a crumb of it. I laid out their sandwiches, some fruit, and a large bag of hula hoops. I hoped it would entice them to eat if they could see it all before them. But it just invited other visitors to join our picnic. What felt like a swarm of seagulls gathered in the sky above us. They were circling aggressively. It reminded me of a scene from the film "The Birds", and I felt quite scared of them in that moment. I was thinking of scenes in the movie where they nearly pulled the actress's hair out of her head and pecked people's eyes out. I was playing it out in my mind, like that was a possible outcome of our day. I wanted to pack up, but I didn't want to anger them either. I was worried if I made any sudden movements, they'd go for my children. I remembered my sister talking about how greedy and determined they could be. Once, when she'd been living in Wales, she'd had a whole sandwich stolen straight from her hand by one of those seagulls' vicious relations.

They were making loud cawing noises, like they were discussing amongst themselves the best means of attack. I was also thinking of the book "The Lighthouse Keeper's Lunch." It had been a beloved children's story that my P2 teacher had read to us innumerable times. I remembered the lengths the seabirds in that story would go to, just to get food. They were crafty and they knew how to remove covers from wicker baskets and how to intimidate ginger cats that were sent to scare them off.

In other words, I was scared. I started to slowly pack up the food, trying not to make any sudden movements. They were flying in like a fleet of army planes by then and I was waiting for them to launch their attack. At best, I thought they'd poop on us; at worst, I wondered if they'd gouge out eyeballs. I was regretting watching classic horror films in that moment. Even if the special effects had been poor, the message remained the same in my mind – birds could be dangerous.

One of them swooped down and stole a Hula Hoop, clutching it in its beak like it was gold. I didn't know that birds liked Hula Hoops, but I guess if you're hungry enough, you'll eat anything. I later learned from a friend that certain birds are like vultures: they'll eat any old scraps. My friend used to leave a feast for them on her windowsill. Apparently, they enjoyed eating whole eggs and sausages. I didn't realise they were carnivores, but apparently vegetarianism wasn't for them. I hoped the seagulls wouldn't cross over from carnivorous to murderous. I managed to pack up the food, the kids, the blanket and put everything back into the pram. As soon as we moved an inch from our spot on the ground, the birds descended and devoured every remaining crumb. So much for our tranquil, beach-side picnic, I thought. Why do the best laid designs never work out? Especially when you bring kids into the equation.

Northern Irish weather isn't the most favourable to picnics, but that wasn't the main problem that day. Future picnics were less plagued by crazed birds, but we've had quite a few in the car when we got caught out in a downpour.

Speaking of things not going to plan when kids are in tow, that reminds me of a memory from my own childhood. We were on a family holiday in Jersey. I must have been about eight years old, and my sister was five. We were visiting the zoo and my parents decided to stop in the canteen for lunch. The place was hiving; I have never seen a restaurant so jam-packed before. It was one of those places where you wait to get served at the counter and then take your seat after you've been served. There was only one empty table left and someone had left a coat lying on the windowsill next to it. It looked unoccupied. There was no food sitting on the table, so we all sat down with our lunch. Suddenly, seemingly out of nowhere, the owner of the coat emerged. He was an angry French man. His wife and son stood sheepishly behind him. I could feel the anger coming off him like vibrations from a shark. It was a horrible feeling. He forced his tray onto the table we were sitting at and knocked everything of ours off the tabletop and onto our knees. Glasses and plates shattered around us. My sister and I were shocked. I just remember my mum speaking very quick French to him and my dad complaining about the fact he'd done that in front of kids. A lovely English family took us under their wings and looked after us while my parents got the restaurant staff involved. The guy ended up being escorted from the premises by the police. I was really shaken up by it, even though, as an adult, now I just regard him as a hot-headed Frenchman with no self-control. When you're a kid, that stuff seems bigger than life itself. Thankfully, I haven't encountered any strangers that rageful with my own kids, but it does always feel like prettily planned out days always involve some sort of hiccup when carried out in real life.

The idyllic version you hold in your head of days out with your kids rarely lives up to the fantasy. Sometimes, it surprises you and you end up making different memories, or you do get one of those rare days when everyone is in good spirits, and nothing goes disastrously wrong. Maybe they stand out as being so special because they are so isolated. I remember one picnic in particular when the sun was blazing down. We went to the seaside for a birthday celebration for my daughter. We had one of those picnics where every detail is attended to, but without the stress of the preparation. It just fell into place. That might be the first time I've ever used that phrase in my children's lifetimes, come think of it. We found a shaded spot under a tree. Even though the weather was glorious, the beach wasn't too busy. Usually that beach is swarming with people at the first sign of sunlight. I guess it does have that perfect combination for parents of a beach, playground and accessible toilet (albeit, about an eighth of a mile away in what is probably, a private cricket ground – but it's still far superior to a port-a-loo or peeing behind a tree.)

We installed ourselves in that secluded spot and the kids happily frolicked in the grass and ate the picnic over a couple of hours. We were at that stage in our family when the adults still outnumbered the kids, so we took it in turns to take them to the playground and there were moments of pure peace for the adults too; all that was missing was a bottle of prosecco. I've never been able to recreate that day, try as I might. Yes, there have been many more beautiful moments, but things rarely come together like that. Life doesn't slot together that simply. I always use that day as a reference point for the type of life I'm trying to create with my kids, and we do have many moments like it, if not full days. It just feels like someone's mood tends to get in the way. It's hard to have a nice day when someone is lying on the floor screeching. Although, I can hardly talk because my tantrums aren't much better.

Sometimes your grumpiness comes out in public. I'm always telling my kids off in public. Sometimes, it invites unwanted comment or looks from prissy parents. They would never tell their kids off in public; they save their criticism for behind closed doors – unless of course, they belong to that breed of parent that never say a cross word. I don't know how such people exist, but I've witnessed it. They have a saccharine tone in which they address their children. It's like whenever you talk to a cute dog and your voice takes on a new quality – the "coochie-coo" voice. I don't understand how they keep that up all the time without having a nervous breakdown, but I guess they must manage it. That, or they suppress their own feelings until old age and then it all comes out as a nasty tirade in the old people's home – probably directed at a caring nurse with a limited command of the English language and an inability to verbally defend themselves.

On one occasion, the kids had been as hyper as hyenas all day and they didn't follow a single instruction. There are two levels of not listening in the life of a parent – the first is extremely irritating but harmless, the second is extremely irritating but dangerous. This fell into the second category. We were at the seaside, and we were on a particularly rocky beach. The tide was in, and each rock had a moist coating of seaweed. The girls insisted on jumping on every single rock, even ones that were protruding from water. I was grasping both their hands for dear life and trying to herd them like they were a much more obedient species, like cattle. Of course, it wasn't working, so I started barking orders instead. That doesn't work either, but sometimes it's a release for the adult, if nothing else. Sometimes, if you're under great strain and you're stuck in a situation, the only thing left to do is shout.

I demanded that the girls get off the slippery rocks and come to my side so I could speak to them. They continued to blank me. It's a special skill they have that they seem to reserve just for me. Finally, I'd had enough, so I pulled them aside and shouted, "you run off one more time on me, I'm walking off and leaving you here." The words alone sounded dramatic, but the growl in which I said them made them sound even worse. As I turned around, a large group of people were standing behind me. They had stopped in their tracks, and they were regarding me with deep judgement. A couple of them were elderly ladies, so I hoped they'd understand. But I guess they saved their spankings for behind closed doors when that was the recommended method of dealing with children. I wished the sand under my feet would turn to quicksand and swallow me whole. People always say if you embarrass yourself in front of a stranger, at least you'll probably never see them again in your entire life. But Northern Ireland is as small as a piss pot, and I have very distinctive hair. I knew they'd probably end up being one of the families whose children attended the same schools as mine, or relatives of the teachers, or grandparents of my daughter's next best friend. Life likes to laugh at you like that sometimes. As I recounted the story later, I realised the humour in it, but at the time, I was just seeing fiery red.

Sometimes, as a parent, you hear the sound of your own voice and think "what have I become?" or "when did I become such an unbearable nag?" But then your kids wake you during the night for the seventh consecutive year and you realise that the lack of sleep might have a lot to do with it.

Chapter Eleven – Storytelling in your Sleep.

Now and again, I'll meet some poor parent that understands my plight. Lack of sleep is maddening. There is a reason it has been used as a torture method for prisoners of war. I wonder if they feel the same loss of sanity that sleep-deprived mums do. It would make you say anything, agree to anything, especially when you're half asleep. My kids like to wake me before the sunrise. They have energy the second their eyelids flip open and their feet touch the floor. I never thought the sound of a descent from a ladder would fill me with such dread, but I never thought of bunkbeds and having children that didn't like to stay in them.

I have never been a morning person. I always thought I was reasonably cheerful – when I'm not in a bad mood, at least, but my mum always says there is no point in having a conversation with me first thing in the morning. Grumpiness aside, you're just not going to get anything remotely coherent or interesting from me. Coffee first, conversation later, in my opinion. I need fuel to put me in the mood to talk. That's why I dread running into someone that wants to have a highly developed conversation on the morning school run. I'm not wakeful enough for that yet. Some people are highly productive first thing in the morning, but I'm like a zombie until I've been up for about three hours and the shock of waking up has finally worn off.

For a long time, my kids loved having stories read to them first thing in the morning. I love reading to them too; in fact it's probably my favourite activity to do with them. There's nothing I love more than sitting on our reading cushions together and getting stuck into their new copy of the Beano or whatever selection of library books they have chosen that week. I just wish I'd set limits on reading or made designated parts of the day "independent reading" time. They like to land in when I'm still asleep, always before six thirty and with every hard backed book they own. They deposit them on my bed, always with the sharp corners meeting my head. I'm still too sleepy to really complain. They open the book and push it under my chin while I'm still lying down. "Read, Mummy, read!" they exclaim in their cheery morning voices. I don't know how to say no to that; I don't want to discourage their love of reading. It's one of the ways in which I've been too soft, and it feels too late to correct it now.

Whenever I try to read when I'm still asleep, I speak a language I didn't know existed. It's either indecipherable or I string together words that don't make any sense together. I've told them wild tales that have made them laugh hysterically, but none of them were stories I consciously pieced together. I held books in front of me – books of which I knew every word, but I changed them into ridiculous versions that in no way resembled the originals. I never realise until my kids start laughing at me and telling me none of it makes any sense. But that's what they deserve I think, for expecting me to read fluently before 7AM. I always thought I loved reading at any hour of the day or night, but apparently not first thing in the morning. Still, kids never pick up on subtle clues – or clanging ones either, so they didn't suggest we just continue with the story when I was fully conscious. They just keep scolding me for being so silly and sleepy and insist upon waking me up. A pair of matchsticks wedged under my eyelids would be very welcome at such moments.

Years ago, I started a tradition of reading before bedtime before my kids understood a word I was saying. I love having little rituals like that. I can still remember my mum reading to my sister and me on some pillows down the side of her wardrobe. It felt like we had our own little reading nook. I remember howling with laughter at "The Twits" and "Boy" and other Roald Dahl masterpieces. My kids enjoy the same books now, but they would never sit next to me while I read something as lengthy as that. They call such novels "bedtime novels," because they want to read The Beano while they're sitting on my knee, and they want to use longer stories as a way to help them drift off to sleep. I don't know if they find them soothing or boring, but it does always lull them to sleep, eventually. The problem is they don't know how to sleep without it now. I've made a rod for my own back, as my mum would say. They might have many treasured memories of us reading together, or it might just be completely taken for granted. Sometimes when you do something every day for your kid, it takes the magic out of it. It's like a family member you see too often or a kind of sweets you sicken yourself with. You don't have time to yearn for it or build it up in your mind as something to look forward to – it's just "there" all the time.

It's got to the point now that I've almost stopped enjoying reading children's classics. I get fifteen chapters into The Jungle Book, and I start to think about getting up. My arse is practically blue from the amount of contact it's had with the floor and then one of my kids stirs. "Keep reading," they say. I start into chapter sixteen, wishing I'd never started in the first place. I wonder in those moments if I should have become one of those parents that send their kids to bed with an iPad. It's not that different than me reading my Kindle before I conk out, I reason. But no, I decided I wanted my kids to be avid readers before they could even hold their heads up, so I keep the tradition going. I just wish they'd learn to sleep by themselves. It's something I hope to achieve before they reach middle age. I can picture my daughter still taking up the other half of my bed when she's forty years old. I didn't plan to do co-sleeping, and yet, here we are, seven years later. My bed practically has a daughter shaped imprint on her half of the mattress.

I'm sure my kids can sense when I'm about to relax and they feel an urge to interrupt it. They know the exact moment when I'm drifting off to sleep or when I've sat down on the sofa with a cup of tea after a long day of loading laundry and continually shouting them to stop shouting. I have always loved that feeling when you finally fall into bed when you're truly tired. Maybe everyone does. It's a delicious feeling at the end of a long day. I love when the mattress feels supple as it holds your exhausted body, and the duvet feels fluffy and comforting, keeping reality's chill out. I always loved hiding in bed. It felt like a hiding place from the rest of the world. But now, my children know exactly where my hiding place is, and they have no qualms about repeatedly invading it.

I don't know if this is how sleep feels to other people, but I'll describe the sensation I get. You've got comfortable, your brain has finally tuned out the mental monologue, the list of to-dos that you can never quite conquer, and you start to slip away into a safer world. I get a bit light-headed as it's happening, but it's not a bad feeling; it's like a release from the day's stresses. I feel like I'm gently being tipped off the plane of consciousness, like an insect encouraged off a piece of paper and back into their natural, wild home. One second later and I'll be fully submerged in sleep. That is the exact moment when the call comes. My daughter has a particular talent for catching me right at that second. "Mummy," she yells, "Mummy!" I jump out of my sleep and sit up in shock. It's a horrible feeling, like waking up to the fact that you're in a building that's about to collapse and it's too late to get out. "Mummy!" she continues calling. My sleepy brain soothes me for a second, telling me that perhaps if I wait a second longer, she'll drift off to sleep again. Maybe, I tell myself, hopefully, she was never fully awake to begin with – she was just sleep-talking and dreaming. I feel a bit jealous of her ability to freely do that. My angry, tired- self visualises the future lie-ins of hers that I plan to interrupt in the teenage years. Maybe that's why some parents are so regimented about their kids having to get up, even when it's the weekend. They had no sleep when their kids were kids and it's time for retaliation.

I have probably spent more nights in my kids' beds than I have in my own since having them. One is in the top bunk. I remember once on holiday, I had to sleep in a top bunk. I was scared to put the kids in it in case an accident happened. It wasn't a regular bunk bed; it was a bed on stilts that almost touched the vaulted ceiling. It stood about eight feet high and had no barriers around it – just a ladder so you could reach it. On the first night there, my kids called me from my sleep, and I went to step out of it as you would a bed at floor level. Thankfully, I realised right before I took the plunge, or we might have spent that holiday in A&E.

Back to my kids' beds at home – I find my daughter's bed quite comfortable, but I would never admit that to her. My kids tell me every night that they are either sick or have had a nightmare. When I was a kid, I had terrifying nightmares every night, so I prefer to play it safe and take their complaints seriously. There's nothing worse as a kid than lying in a dark room, trying to get back to sleep after a dream that's still playing on your mind. A night light just doesn't cut it in such situations. But kids are smart, and I suspect mine have just learnt how to play me. They know the magical keys to unlocking access to my bed and they use them each and every night. Despite the fact they claim to be sick most nights of their lives, they're always in good health the next day and the first thing they ask is "what are we doing today?" I feel like saying "watching me with my face pressed against the table, catching up on the sleep I missed out on last night," but I know they'd never let me do that either.

My younger daughter is particularly tricky when it comes to sneaking into my bed. She appears mere minutes after I've decided to retire for the night. She tries to make out that she stumbled into my room without any recollection of her arrival, but in the morning, I have to laugh when I notice she has brought her favourite selection of teddies, her blankie and her water bottle, all positioned as they were when I originally tucked her into her own bed at bedtime. It's clear that there was nothing accidental about it. Still, she upholds the story that she doesn't know how she came to be in my bed. She must be a very organised sleep-walker; that's all I have to say.

My older daughter doesn't get up as much during the night. She saves her getting up for the moment I decide to sit down to relax for the evening instead. It was much the same when the girls still napped. It was like they had arranged a schedule to ensure I was as deprived of rest as possible – like a long-standing practical joke that I definitely didn't find funny. I can always depend on my daughter calling me as soon as I lie down in a warm bath, or I start into my yoga routine. After the part where the lady instructs you to lie down, release all tension and get into breathing at a slower pace, that's exactly when my daughter calls me – then or whenever I have just mastered a difficult yoga pose and I'm precariously balanced there.

"I'm coming in a minute" never pacifies her either. She always wants everything to have happened yesterday. Waiting is not a strong point of any member of our family, and they have inherited the genetic impatience problem, but it seems to be to an even greater degree. She just continues screaming my name, even when I'm in the middle of going to the bathroom and getting to her that second just isn't physically possible. Physical impossibility has never been something my kids have understood. I wonder if all mothers experience this. But when I explain it to others, some of them just look blankly at me – that gaping goldfish look that tells you they don't have a clue what you're talking about.

It seems to me that there are two kinds of children – the calm and collected and the demanding and danger-seekers. Mine most definitely slot into the second category. There are so many good things about that. I don't think anyone has ever made me laugh as much as my kids have before. They're hilarious and energetic and inspiring. Their creativity feeds mine. When I'm in a creative slump and I see them enjoying a project they've started all on their own initiative, it fires me up to try again. I never would have produced as much as I have in the last few years if they hadn't been there to nudge me along. Having such limited alone time makes you use it more wisely too. When you know you have an hour's window to write your novel, you make sure you don't procrastinate. You fill every second of that time with something valuable – or try to at least – even just for your own sense of satisfaction. If you had a life of holidays, you'd probably never go anywhere or do anything, but if you know you only have a limited number of days, you want to make plans for them. It's the same idea.

I try to get her settled in her bed with some magazines or books, if she promises not to be loud and wake her sister. I tell her she must stay in bed and if she does, she can read until she gets sleepy. I leave the landing light on for her so she can see, without waking her sister. As soon as I get downstairs, I get involved in something I've been saving up all day, something that has made me look forward to bedtime as I fantasised about the peace I'd find there. But peace and my children are repellents. I set my book down, or my writing, or the chocolate bar I'm sneaking when I hear a bump upstairs. I hope that perhaps she has fallen into a deep sleep and has dropped one of her books onto the floor in the process. But that is never the case. It is always something that requires intervention. The bump becomes something that sounds like furniture being shifted. It sounds like moving day has arrived for the family next door. But I know it's coming from my own home – sadly, I can't make it the responsibility of the people on the other side of the wall. I rush upstairs and scold her for not remaining quietly reading in her bed.

She takes one of two positions – she either pretends she hasn't moved from her bed, or she claims she only got up to go to the bathroom. It sounded like she was fitting one – never mind making a quick trip to it. While she's telling me these excuses, I mean, explanations, she shouts at the top of her voice, like she's talking to someone on the other side of a very busy street.

"Shhhh," I say. "You'll wake your sister."

We then proceed to have a lesson in whispering – talking about what it is and how to do it. At 9.30 pm, I don't have the patience left to tackle something like that. It feels like something that should be inbuilt, that I shouldn't have to pass on. My daughter acts like she completely understands the meaning of the word "whispering," after a lengthy discussion about it. As soon as I wish her goodnight, she continues to call me at full volume, shouting questions after me as I go, like a string of bullets that chase me downstairs. I repeat this process until she finally succumbs to sleepiness. As soon as I finally get her settled for what I hope will be the night, I can count upon her sister waking up. It's like a relay race I can never win because it never ends, and I always end up with the bloody baton.

Sometimes, I'll talk about it to a friend of mine, and they tell me that their kids have been sleeping through the night since they were one. I always look at them like they're some sort of magical unicorn-like creature. How have they cracked the code I've fail to find? They've mastered their child's sleep solution and I feel incredibly envious. I have moments of considering getting in contact with the producers of Supernanny, but I suspect even she would be at a loss for what to do with my kids.

Chapter Twelve – What to do with the Masterpieces

In my sleep deprived state, it's a wonder we manage to do anything, but your body somehow adapts to whatever torture it endures. I find it easier to go out with my kids sometimes than to attempt staying at home. Whenever we do spend a day at home, you'd need to bring in industrial cleaners by the end of it to tackle the mess. I've lost count of the number of fights in which I've had to intervene. I feel my stress levels soaring, and the only thing that lowers them is a change of scenery – an open space for my kids to run off a little of their everlasting energy.

We have always been familiar with every playpark in the area, every possible walk, every place of interest. People sometimes ask me how we fit so much into our day. It's because it starts at 6am and finishes when the next day begins. My kids are also the kinds of creatures that find destructive ways to entertain themselves if you don't get in there with a craft first. We have made so many crafts over the years, I don't know where to store them anymore. One of the problems is that I genuinely believe that each and every creation my kids produce is a work of art. I always find something cute in each piece, or something unique, or some reason why it can't end up in the recycling bin. Sometimes, I discreetly ask other mums what they do with all their kids' artwork and most mouth to me "straight into the blue bin." I wish I was less sentimental with their creations at times. We have a huge hamper on top of the kitchen cupboards that doesn't close properly because paper is coming out of its mouth. On top of that, I have a few box files in the same predicament, shoved away in the kitchen cupboards. Then, the teachers send home all their work from the school year, and the girls insist on showing it to me, piece by piece. They treasure every single one – even if it's a cut and paste page that they haven't had time to colour in because they were probably too busy talking to their "BFF's."

One day, I hope I'll have the discernment to figure out what I'm obliged to keep and what I can rid myself of, so we have the illusion of space around us. That's something that never exists in our living quarters. Sometimes, I plan to have major clear-outs, but the effects are always short-lasting. It only takes a couple of days for the paper piles to mount up again. No one ever told me about the amount of paperwork I would receive as a parent. Putting aside the vast quantities of artwork and the schoolwork sent home that my children have toiled over all academic year, there are the letters. There are medical reviews, reminders about eye appointments, lists of what needs sent into school that week, permission slips, school calendars, child protection booklets, absence policies, music lesson forms, fundraising plans. I could go on and on. I have. But I don't know what other parents do with it all. They must be fearlessly ruthless or else they have a highly organised filing system. Maybe they rent storage space specifically to accommodate the parental paper trail, or maybe they have regular backyard bonfires and manage to retain all the information in their much higher functioning cerebral quarters. Whatever they do, it feels like they have a better answer to it all than I do. But maybe that's something every parent thinks – every self-doubting parent, at least. It's easy to think that everyone else always has it figured out, because you're only ever catching snapshots of their day. Maybe other parents even have those thoughts about you sometimes, when you aren't shrieking like a banshee at your kids for jumping on your collapsed furniture.

But I know I've also had moments of harsh judgement from others. They mightn't always say it aloud, but you can tell they're thinking it. It's usually at a moment where you've lost control of the whole operation – somewhere that you can't immediately get out of, but you desperately wish you could, like a slow-moving grocery till queue. It's always when one or both of my kids is having a "moment" that the granny in front of me decides to pay for her entire food shop in pennies, or someone decides to leave the queue to go in search of an essential item they forgot to pick up on their first tour of the shop. They don't return for twenty minutes, but because they are mid-transaction, no one else can be served in the meantime. We're all just hemmed in behind them like fenced in sheep butting up against each other. My kids always butt the most.

I can recall one incident where my daughter threw herself onto the shop floor when I had an almost filled trolley and refused to get back up again. The huge shop acted like a megaphone for her screams. It was one of those huge warehouses with the vaulted ceilings that always seems to find a deathly quiet when you're trying to mask your child's howls. For some reason, the music wasn't even playing that day. Each person that passed me looked at me like I was burying a body in the middle of the aisle. Maybe those looks are just looks of shock, or confusion – people trying to make sense of a loud situation that they've suddenly become a part of, without their consent. But when you're that stressed out, you interpret every single look as one of severe judgement.

My kids can be very impulsive at times, but then again, so can I. Sometimes the things that your kids have inherited from you are the things that annoy you the most. Maybe it's because you couldn't master the qualities within yourself, never mind being able to work out how you might master it in miniature, but often enhanced format.

Food shopping with kids is stressful in general. Even when they were both babies that could sit side by side in a double trolley. (When we found one. Finding one of those was like finding a jewel in a toilet bowl.) The problem was that if the shop's free fruit basket hadn't been replenished, it started us off on a bad note. Those free oranges and apples saved my sanity, even if most of them ended up in a baby wipe handbag I'd fashioned when picking them up off the floor. I feel sorry for post-covid parents now that don't have those little luxuries. However, as soon as the last bite or the last pitch was taken, the peace was gone. It didn't matter whether you used the straps or not; my kids always managed to get out of them anyway. When most kids couldn't figure out how to put the circle shape in the shape sorter's circular hole, they were hatching elaborate escape plans. They never stayed put in their seats. They always somehow made it into main part of the trolley and sat on everything soft. We'd end up with a loaf of bread that looked like a squashed piece of clay before we even made it to the till.

When we finally did make it there, it was like reaching a secret door that could have opened onto heaven or hell. The only way to find out was to step through it. As I attempted to pack bags, making sure that everything had been scanned and wasn't squirreled away under my kids' bums, they would decide to stand up in the back of the trolley and try to swing back into their original seats. There are three types of till operators – the first finds everything kids do funny, even if they were contemplating matricide, probably; the second scowls if they do so much as smile at them, and the third shares their sympathy for you. "I had two of my own, but they're grown up now. It's not easy, is it? You've got your hands full," they'd say, kindly. That was the kind of comment that was most appreciated. It translated to "you aren't a walking failure with kids as crazed as loosed zoo animals."

But I rarely seemed to encounter such a soul. I got a fair split of the first two. I almost preferred the scowlers because they weren't egging my kids on in. The other kind of shop assistant smiles sweetly and laughs at their mischief and then I feel like a monster. I can't see the humour in it in those moments – maybe in a few years, looking back on it, with the safe distance of time, and no risk of running into the same situation again. Yes, now I can see they were being rascals, but at the time, I just didn't have enough hands to manage that while I tried to extract my debit card from my disorganised purse. When we go shopping now, there are constant suggestions made about what we should buy, and it most definitely increases the food bill threefold, but at least they aren't climbing like chimpanzees on top of the shopping. I still always manage to squish the loaf though.

Chapter Thirteen – Rave Reviews

There is a lady whose videos I regularly watch. She talks about her kids' highly developed empathy, and I can see it in action. When she was sick, she said they helped to care for her. They brought her water, kept her company, and did the laundry for her. Sometimes I wish I'd been better at being consistent where cleaning was concerned. My kids tidy their toys every day, when prompted to do so. But they are generally messy in between such moments. As I scrub the floors and get the kitchen looking better than it has in weeks, they're busy dismantling the living room. It's impossible to clean quicker than the rate at which they create mess. Maybe that's just a part of it – and a part of their personalities. They're always creating something, even if that thing can only be referred to as "a mess."

As a kid, I remember my mum instructing me to dust everything, and I wasn't happy about it. I didn't do it happily, but I did do it thoroughly. Maybe my mum was just better at overseeing the whole thing and making sure we didn't miss a spot. I usually give my kids the hoover or duster while I'm working on something else. I thought the point was to delegate and get the work done quicker, but maybe some training needs to be provided first. My daughter's idea of dusting is giving the coffee table a tickle and then returning with the clean cloth, declaring the job done. I send her to redo it, and then I find her ten minutes later, playing with her babies on the floor. It makes me laugh, even though it's irritating. She will do anything do get out of doing work.

One day I was dropping her off at school for the day in P1 and I said "have a great day."

"Probably not," was her come back.

"Why do you say that?"

"All I do is work, work, work," she said, rolling her eyes.

I wonder what else she expects to do in school.

Which reminds me of her first parent teacher's meeting this year. I walked into the room with trepidation. I knew she'd been hard work (and yes, that's hard work – not hard at work) all summer and I was scared the teacher's story would match my own.

"I had to move her away from her friend because she wouldn't stop talking," the teacher said. "She's sitting in front of my desk now."

When I was in school, that seat was reserved for the especially naughty. I sensed that there was more to the story than she was sharing with me. I just nodded and waited for her to elaborate.

"She shouts out in class quite a bit," she said.

I could feel myself reddening. I'd never been someone that liked to draw attention to themselves in school – especially not in a bad way. It was hard to believe that I had a child that was the exact oppositive to me.

"What does she shout out?" I asked. I only half wanted to hear the answer.

"She groans if we've done something before and shouts "we've already done this – this is boring – why do we have to do it again?"

I was mortified. I've always hated the words "bored" and "boring" and banned them from our house, and here my child was, parading around in public, proclaiming everything boring in front of her peers.

"I just tell her – we have to repeat it to practise it, so we can get better at it, but she isn't keen to do it."

I got a sudden flashback from the previous year, when her teacher had informed me that her work could be "scruffy" and that she rushed through things. (Not that I needed to be informed of that; I saw her homework book every week and was well-acquainted with its grubby, grey fingerprinted layout.

She'd always needed more than a nudge to colour in properly and to form her letters with care. She'd never enjoyed colouring for pleasure. When most kids, I assumed, were getting stuck into a colouring book, (because if they weren't – why did the shops even bother to keep selling them?) she was always onto the next thing. Nothing has changed in that respect. She asked me yesterday whilst holding an ice-cream she had just started eating if we could go out for dinner. She doesn't even enjoy the treat she has while she's eating it. I think the pleasure for her lies in stacking up her future earnings where promised treats are concerned.

It didn't feel like my daughter's teacher had much to say about her behaviour that was positive. Maybe that was why her most recent parent-teacher meeting made me so proud. I don't worry too much about academic achievement, particularly at the age of six, but her behaviour sounded like that of another child this time around. I almost wondered if she'd got wires crossed somewhere and given my daughter's report to a different parent.

"She's just a good wee girl – she's a credit to you," her teacher said. "And she's great craic – she's always got a smile for everybody and she's a kind friend."

That was all I wanted to hear. I'm not driving her to outperform her peers with her ABC's. So long as she's kind to others and helpful towards her teacher, I'm happy.

Sometimes, that's the good thing about receiving mixed reviews for something: when you expect the worst and then hear the best, it sounds even sweeter. I wish I felt the same way about getting mixed reviews of my books.

Chapter Fourteen – Leggings and a Stained T-Shirt

I knew the day would come when I would no longer approve of my kids' clothing choices. I just didn't think it would arrive so soon. It isn't in the way I expected either. For years, when the girls were little, people used to always compliment them on their clothes. They wore cute little outfits of dresses and matching cardigans. They had Clarks buckle shoes that seemed to stay mostly scuff-free despite the regularity of our trips to the playground. We'd practically taken up residence there during the toddler years.

"She looks like a wee doll," a friendly stranger would comment. "She matches you with her outfit," another would say.

I have loved dresses for my entire adult life, and I like to get dressed up for no reason. It just gives me a confidence boost and I feel more positive about the day ahead of me. I had just conveniently forgotten about my football years. In primary school, I didn't give a fig about what I looked like. Comfort and practicality for playing on the football pitch were my only concerns. I never thought about whether I looked "nice." I just wanted what the other kids were wearing – zip bottomed Adidas tracksuit bottoms and a turtleneck, probably. At irregular intervals, my mum produces all the pre 2000 photos. I cringe as soon as I see them. She showed them to my boyfriend recently and I was surprised he didn't break up with me on the spot. In most of the pictures, I was wearing cycling shorts with pulled up ankle socks. I looked blissfully happy and brutally unfashionable. I just didn't even have an awareness of it. I wouldn't be seen dead in any of that clobber now, so I'm glad someone else disposed of the shorts. I know the fashions of the nineties were different than those now, but there was still no excuse for it. When I remember that, I realise I can't be too hard on my kids about wearing what they want to wear. They have developed their own styles of late and none of them include dresses with matching accessories.

Why do kids reach the age of six and suddenly want to wear practical clothes. They just want a pair of leggings, a stained T-shirt and a hoody. They don't want to look pretty – that or they just have a different definition of prettiness by then. I've stopped buying what I consider to be "nice" clothes for my kids. I learned my lesson about that the hard way.

A while ago, I found an independent clothing store online that sold organic clothes. The prints were all so quirky and some of their clothes were even reversible. I decided to splash out and buy my kids a few things from it. When they arrived, the clothes looked even better to me in real life. One was a shocking blue coloured skirt with an intricate paisley print and high-quality cord fabric. I told myself the girls would love their items; they always got so excited about getting new things.

But their disappointment was instantly obvious. They wouldn't have chosen the items themselves, and even my demonstration on the reversibility of the pieces didn't sell them on what I'd bought. I kept moving the items of clothing to the tops of their drawers, reminding them that they were there and that they should be worn. The girls just tossed them aside. I kept finding them, wrinkled and shoved down the side of the chest of drawers. Finally, I admitted defeat and sold the clothes on Vinted. I only got a couple of pounds for them, but that was much better than the thanks my own children had given me.

Now, I've learnt that I just need to let them get on with it. If I'm ever shopping for staples without them, I just have to ask myself the question "what's the last thing I would pick to buy here?" That usually provides me with their dream outfit. They particularly love anything with a mantra printed on it. That's a pet peeve of mine. Statements like "stay positive always" annoy me beyond description. It's too general to actually be applied to lifelike situations, and it's like a pat on the shoulder when you haven't even asked for one. Whoever comes up with the lines for those clothing lines has an enviable job in my view. I wish someone would pay me to come up with trite compositions and print them off. Oh, wait -

Chapter Fifteen – Librarians like their Windows

One of my favourite things to do with my kids is to go to the library. Libraries are a hugely underrated commodity. They're a free resource that allow you to keep your kids entertained for hours. A few years ago, a friend introduced us to a library that I didn't even know existed. It's at the back of a rough housing estate and it's hidden away from the main road. I'd never seen it advertised anywhere, and it has a delipidated look to it from the outside. If you happened to be in the area, you could easily drive past it without really noticing it. But it's a gold mine. The basement of the library is entirely dedicated to kids. The librarian that runs it is one of the loveliest people I've ever met. She's like the librarian that introduces Matilda to her love of reading in the film, only she introduces us to free events and juice and biscuits, which are just as important, really. Pre-covid, they even had a small soft play area that my kids loved to climb on and dismantle, and no one ever complained.

I like using our closest library too, but it's more compact and you get the sense that you're under everyone's feet in there. There are elderly people there, in search of a quiet reading spot, and when you barge in with your kids, they never look happy to see you. The adult and children's sections are adjacent to one another, due to a lack of space, so I'm constantly shushing my kids. And if you ever have a forgotten book that's still on loan, they make sure to tell you. At least they've done away with fines for overdue books now. I love to read, but if I get a book out of the library, it will probably take me close to three months to make the time to finish it. It's hard to get immersed in a story when someone is constantly calling your name and asking you for something – pulling you back into the reality you've striven to escape.

The first time we set foot in the friendly library, the lady gave us a warm greeting and introduced us to the other librarians on shift. She was making a seasonal wall display and she got the girls to help her to blue tac everything to the wall. They loved every second of it. She has a way of making everyone feel valued and that their presence is important there. That's something you rarely find in customer service now, so when you do, it really stands out. The place has been a lifesaver to us over the years. We haven't had huge amounts of money to throw around us, so it's great to have an activity that is always free. There have been so many moments of distress and grief that I've lived through with kids and it was a sanctuary for us. We walked in and the librarian got my kids some stickers and colouring pages and some juice, biscuits and coffee for me. She encouraged my writing and another librarian there even put my book in the libraries. The librarian has only ever shown us her kindly face. We ran into her one day outside the library. It turns out her son only lives two streets away from us and she was dog-sitting for him at the time.

One day, we ventured into the library around the 12th of July. There's a huge disused car park right beside it and it was one of the sites being used for the bonfires. There was a stack of wooden crates the size of a building and teenagers were sitting all over it, perched on every side, smoking, drinking, taking drugs and generally being what the police would probably class as "antisocial." The librarian was her usual jolly self when we walked in, but with a hint of irritableness.

"Them'uns are getting on my wick," she said, nodding in the direction of the crew outside.

The library had got new windows in the previous year after an incident that led to the windows being smashed. The librarian treasured her new windows. It had taken months for them to finally get fitted. They were her pride and joy. The teenagers outside kept kicking their football, so it hit the windows hard. It was also causing the Roald Dahl display they'd just stuck to the windows to shake. She was livid. She stormed out of the library, and I could hear her from inside screaming at them. It was funny in a way – seeing that other side of her, but she was so protective of her library, and they were being disgustingly disrespectful. I resumed looking for books, hoping the windows wouldn't come in around us. We all laughed to each other – the few of us that were in the building. It was one of those moments when you realise the positioning of the library and the irony of trying to deliver a valuable resource to people that are incapable of appreciating it. She came back in, closing the door decisively behind her. The kids did seem to pipe down after that. They stopped kicking the football at the windows at least. I've always admired people like her – they're so genuine and kind, but they have a side that people know not to mess with. They manage to strike fear into the hearts of others when needed. I don't think I've ever been like that. Even when I try to be stern with my kids, they laugh at me, like they think I'm just doing an impression of someone strict, but not really carrying it off.

I always find it strange when people are sensitive about their kids getting told off. I delight in mine getting told off by someone other than me. It makes my day when they have ignored my requests hundreds of times that day and then a stranger intervenes and they come running to me, looking for sympathy. Sometimes they just need to hear the same complaint in a different voice to yours. Every day when we went to my older daughter's school for the drop off and pick up, I had my other daughter in tow. She is really determined when she wants to do something. That's a nice way of putting it. There is a huge grassy bank that the kids all love to play on. I don't know what it is about it – it's just like cartwheel central. During Covid they weren't allowed to go on it, so every morning, I'd give her a stern warning to stay off it – at least it sounded that way in my own head. She'd agree to steer clear until we entered the gates. Then she'd act like we'd never met before. She'd see a friend, and take off, leading them astray too. After what felt like weeks of warning her to stay off it, a male teacher finally approached her and told her to get off it. Of course, she did right away – although the chastisement didn't have any lasting effect. She was back on it the following day, like nothing had ever happened. I remember recounting the story to my parents and my dad saying to her, "you had to get told off by a teacher from another school?!" She just shrugged and did a funny face that told me it hadn't had any effect on her confidence.

During heavy rainfall and in the winter, it becomes too swampy to use, but that's never a deterrent. One day, I was standing talking to the granny of one of her friends when she walked over to me. She had that "I'm in trouble now, but what's the worst she can do?" look on her face. She was covered from head to toe in mud. Every inch of her school uniform was saturated. Her shoes were clogged with mud, and I knew I'd have one hell of a cleaning job to do when I got home. I didn't even know what to say to her. I scolded her, but I couldn't even think of an appropriate punishment for her. The problem is that for most people, such incidents are lessons that teach them not to do the thing again, but my daughter isn't that easily put off something.

"If she was mine, I'd murder her," laughed the lady beside me.

I was so embarrassed; we always seemed to draw attention to ourselves wherever we went, and not for good deeds. Her shoes were so badly caked with mud that she had to wear her trainers for the rest of the week. Her school shoes sat on the radiator for days, but not even that was enough to dry them. She could finally wear them again about a fortnight later.

When things break, my kids always take the attitude of "oh, well, we can just get another one." I have no idea where this originated from because I can't recall replacing a broken item once. I guess I should be glad that they don't have an unhealthy attachment to things – unless of course, I'm planning on making a trip to the charity shop or the dump. My children could own a toy for years and never pick it up, but as soon as you place it near a binbag or mention the possibility of passing it on to someone else, they decide they can't bear to be separated from it. That's why I usually leave clear-outs until they are in school. They are both hoarders. If it was up to them, we'd keep everything that ever passed through our hands – napkins, plastic spoons, ketchup sachets, cardboard packaging. We have a junk box for crafting and sometimes I wonder if I've pushed the recycling idea a bit too much. They can find a use for anything that belongs in the blue bin, and the problem is, they do turn the things into attractive, or at least functional objects, so I don't even feel like I can throw them out.

One time, when they were going through one of their earliest existential question sessions, my mum was babysitting them for me. They'd mentioned death a few times to me, but not in a fearful way – more in a curious way. That night, my mum said they'd brought it up at bedtime. In her eyes, they were truly fearful; in mine, they were employing any technique to dodge bedtime. Apparently, as they were being tucked in for the night, they expressed worry about being parted from their belongings in the afterlife. "Nannie, when we die, can we take our teddies with us?" My mum told them that their teddies would indeed be welcome in heaven. As I write this, I'm understanding why she answered the way she did. It really does pull at your heartstrings when kids say things like that.

"What about our bed, Nannie?"

"Yes, you can take your beds with you."

"What about our toys?"

"Yes, you can take them with you too. You can take the whole house with you," my mum said.

I can see her saying it in my mind, even without having been there. I can picture her saying it in her former drama teacher voice, sweeping arm movements to accompany the statement. She said it seemed to reassure them enough to enable them to sleep anyway. Why do such conversations always come up at the moment when you've left your kids in the care of a family member or babysitter? They never seem to address such topics at bedtime with me. Maybe it's because they know I won't tolerate talking after 7.30pm. When it's your Nannie putting you to bed, you can draw out the bedtime routine for longer than usual. Although, I never would have dared to do that with my grandmother– but she could be a bit of a dragon at times. I can too, so I guess it's genetic or something.

My kids didn't talk about death for a long time after that, so I guess it must have helped; that, or it was never that great of a worry in the first place.

A few weeks later, my younger daughter told my mum she liked the jewelled ring she was wearing.

"Can I have it when you die?" she asked, ruthlessly.

I guess their fear surrounding death only applies when they aren't going to inherit sparkly things because of it.

Chapter Sixteen - Adventures Abroad

I only attempted travelling with my kids when they were little if we had other adults there too. When they were under the ages of one and two, we went to my sister's wedding in Majorca. My mum booked flights before we did. I guess she got a good deal on late night flights or thought it would be a quieter time to travel at. I nearly had heart failure at the thought of it because my kids always went to bed at half seven and any deviation from that produced demon children. I was worried about taking the flight, but at least family were on board, so if things got really bad, I had family to pass the children to, or to at least hide behind. Usually, when you run those scenarios through your mind, you come up with an exaggerated version of the worst outcome, but in that case, I would say my worries were spot on. Of course, they didn't sleep a wink and they cried for the duration of the flight. My mum ended up having to take them in turns to the back of the plane where a lovely steward entertained them. Thank God I didn't try to do it alone. I've always worried too much about disturbing other people, so disrupting an entire flight at midnight was my vision of hell. It was a long three hours and I'd never been gladder to see a successful landing. In fact, I would have taken an unsuccessful one at that stage. There's nothing like your kid having a public meltdown to get you over your fear of flying.

The holiday was much more relaxed than the flight. As my mum always says when we're all together – there are plenty of adults to juggle the kids. The only problem was that they were almost all occupied with the wedding taking place – and rightly so. But while they were making the final preparations and socialising on the bar's terrace, I spent most of the evenings on my hotel balcony chain-smoking and feeling like my head was going to explode. It was a nice environment to have a nervous breakdown in though.

The last time I was abroad before that was before kids. I associated being overseas with sunbathing by the pool and relaxed reading marathons. I even finished Anna Karenina on one holiday to the same destination as the wedding. Gone were those days and they had been replaced with turning the air conditioning up full and trying not to breathe too loudly so my kids would still take their morning nap. They used their travel cots as small soft play areas, bouncing off the sides of the cot. They fussed and made grunting sounds that told me there was no chance of sleep. Getting a nap out of them was basically just putting myself in solitary confinement in the ensuite anyway. It just took the edge off, so there would be fewer tantrums in the late afternoon. The adults were all eating together at 8pm, so we were getting room service that night anyway. At least that meant there were fewer potential public meltdowns, unless people overhearing us on our hotel floor counted. The pool was our saving grace – that, and the breakfast buffet. There are certain benefits that come along with increased stress. My mum let me get my eyelashes dyed and I got out of the room for a couple of drinks one night. But that was the height of my relaxation.

That first trip gave me the bravery to venture further afield alone. By further afield, I mean twenty miles down the road. I rented a holiday cottage near Downpatrick. I was deep in the country, and I'd never stayed anywhere like that before, without streetlights at night. It was spooky after dark and there were a few too many bugs for my liking, but other than that, it was a much easier holiday destination with kids – mainly because I knew if things got really bad, we could always drive back home. I wonder if every parent considers that when booking a holiday for their kids or is that only a consideration when yours are a bit out of control? My kids don't listen to me now, but at that age, it was much worse. There wasn't a bad bone in them, but they were always up to some mischief. Sometimes I'd see other families where a baby was sitting, wearing a sunhat and chewing on a toy, never moving from that one spot on the picnic blanket. I almost felt jealous then, that their parents got to sit down. My bottom never got to touch a seat then, and as soon as I dared to, my kids found a reason to get me up again. I can still remember so many special moments from that trip, like early morning walks on unspoilt beaches. We were the first ones there each day. Then we found the restaurant with an attached playground for kids. They were still at the stage where they had to be supervised on everything, but at least it broke up the meal, letting them run around somewhere other than on the restaurant floor. We found an artist's shop filled with handcrafted treasures that were on sale at reasonable prices. We had ice-cream in the harbour and sunned ourselves in the long stretch of good weather that you never seem to get in Northern Ireland. I had peaceful evenings, when the kids slept deeply after twelve hours of running around in the fresh air. I got to drink wine in the cosy kitchen and write at the old oak table with the heat of the aga warming the floors. There was an open fire and because it was close to my parents' village, they got to join us for dinner one night and for tea in front of the fire. The downsides were the fact the garden wasn't enclosed. It ran in a circle right round the house. The only traffic was the local tractors, but I didn't like to take any chances with my kids, so we ended up running around it the whole time we were there. There was no time to stop and smell the roses that wove through the front picket fence. There was a drop behind a tree at the edge of the lawn that they seemed to be particularly attracted to and the kitchen had two doors leading outside that just felt like they should be perpetually open. We walked in circles until I went from mild irritation to not being able to stand it a second longer, and then we went out for more walking. It didn't matter how high our step count was; it never tired out my kids – at least not until twelve hours later. Putting them to bed wasn't fun either. Once they were asleep, they were ok. There were two bedrooms in the place. One was like a dorm room with about six beds. The other had a double bed with a little glass feature window, lamps and the potential for cosy reads at night after the kids were asleep. But I ended up sleeping in one of the little single beds every night because they wanted me to stay in the room with them. There were a few things about the cottage that were a bit unnerving. There was a wardrobe there that the owner had informed me belonged to his great-great grandfather. It was impressive that it was still standing, but there was something overbearing about it too. It took over the room and it felt like it could house every ghost from the family, it was so deep and cavernous. It was like the wardrobe in The Lion, the Witch and the Wardrobe. I could see why it would give my kids nightmares if left alone in the dark with it. I was more worried about the beams on the ceiling and the cobwebbed corners large enough to contain the webs of fifteen arachnids. I tried not to think about that as I closed my eyes as tightly as they would shut, pretending to my kids that everything was fine and there was nothing to be afraid of in the nineteenth century cottage. It was scary to think of just how much history it could have held in two hundred years. Very old buildings have always made the hairs on my arms stand on end. Maybe it's just one of the sensitivities of an empath, but sometimes I wish my senses were less heightened to things like that. I could remember staying in an old mansion once on the outskirts of Glasgow. I was the only one that seemed to notice that the house was creepy as hell. Even the little kids that lived there and were young enough to barge into my room before breakfast didn't seem perturbed by it.

But this was our first holiday mostly alone and it felt like something to be proud of. People only ever show you snapshots of the moments when they're smiling – real or not. All holidays are composed of good and bad moments, unless you come from one of those families that just always gets along famously and never fights. I've met a couple of them, but usually they do have grievances with each other – they're just all suppressed. At least we aren't like that – my kids annoy me, and I annoy them, but we tell each other directly and then get over it. Despite my pronouncement that we would return to the same cottage for another holiday, we never did. Maybe it was just too much like a work-out with all those doors and the unfenced garden. I still have a pair of earrings from the shop with the work of local artists showcased on every stand. It was an inspiring place to be. I think you need to have places like that near the sea, or everyone that lives there gets cut off from their community and goes a bit mad. It's too easy to fish solo or stay at home in front of the open fire. Although saying that, in the midst of the school run madness, that sounds pretty good to me.

Chapter Seventeen – Cakes to be Proud of

After that, we had a holiday in the Mournes. We were in a lovely cottage at the foothills of the mountains. It was the most beautiful backdrop I'd ever seen, and we could enjoy it all evening, with it being summer and the house having outdoor seating. That was a luxury we still didn't have at home. I would have killed for a garden at the time. That was probably why we went away so much. I was trying to make do by then with a plot of grass out the front of the flat we were living in that was in an unofficial old people's development. I was the only resident there under seventy, and the only one that, likely, had any interest in using our front lawn. But I didn't, most of the time, in case I offended somebody. The independent-living elderly are often easily offended and territorial – even about territory that isn't really theirs. We still made a single snowman there though, the day before we moved out. He was a stumpy little thing with half a body and a cheery face. He was made of so little snow that you couldn't see him from a distance. And by from a distance, I mean from our living room window. Snowman building has always been one of those rites of passage activities you have to experience with your kids. You need to be in the right mood for it though, and it can't take place when you're sick. My kids always have very specific requests; "demands" would be more accurate. They wouldn't have been happy with anything but a carrot nose, so our snowman had the top of a carrot since his face was so small it couldn't even support a baby one.

Back to our holiday – the girls loved the garden in that place. It was more closed in than the other one, so they could explore without me constantly worrying they'd make a break for it. They found a stash of Scooby Doo DVD's and a selection of board games, so they wanted to do that all morning. We played Snakes and Ladders about forty times. Then we went out for the afternoon. When we got back, I started making dinner and they wanted to go into the garden. There was a rock garden there, so I ended up following them around it. They were drawn to it as they are always drawn to danger. Which reminds me of a tangential story that is basically completely unrelated. Please forgive the meandering plot line.

I've always tried to keep everything well out of reach of my kids, especially when they were little. They were always terrible pokers. If they found my body lotion on the bathroom floor, they couldn't resist buttering the bathroom with it. If you left a box of tissues sitting out, they'd tear every tissue to shreds and try to eat them. If you left a snack within reach, they'd act like pigs upon discovering an unsealed and accessible bag of food. That was why I kept sharp things like scissors on the highest shelves of cupboards. I could barely reach them, so I thought it was safe to assume they couldn't either.

One day, I had a visit from our new health visitor. She was a lovely lady - thankfully. Some of the previous ones we'd had were very unpleasant, but she was faultlessly encouraging. It really was a good job she was, because if there was one moment when my kids were going to show a crack in my baby proofing, it would, of course, be at that moment. I was having a casual chat on the sofa with the health visitor, who was complimenting my décor, saying how much it suited us. My kids were wandering around downstairs. They have never been able to stay in the one room for long, never mind the one spot. As we were chatting, they had obviously been coming up with one of their masterplans in the kitchen. They walked in, a minute later, holding a pair of scissors. It wasn't even one of those kid-safe pairs with the safety latch or the plastic kind that couldn't cut play doh. It was one of those giant pairs that looks like you're wielding a weapon when you pull them from the drawer. They weren't carrying them in the way you're meant to carry scissors either. I gasped and jumped up to grab them from them. It was ridiculous that something that had never happened before that day had to happen during the half-hour health visitor visit. The health visitor was good about it though.

"The council carry out home safety checks if you have children – free of charge," she said. "Would you be interested in one?"

I wasn't, but I didn't feel like saying that would help me in that moment.

"Sure, what do I need to do?"

"I'll sign you up for one and they'll give you a call to schedule it."

I nodded appreciatively. We went for a quick walk around the downstairs, probably so she could do a risk assessment. When she found my cleaning products lined up on a tall shelf in a closed off room, she gave me a nod of approval. "Well done, Mum," she said. I felt like maybe the blot I'd made on my copy book was fading a little.

I hoped she realised the scissor moment was just a slip up. I hadn't known how my kids had even got hold of the scissors. I asked myself if they'd been left sitting out by mistake. When we walked through the kitchen, we could see that a chair had been moved away from the kitchen table and over to the kitchen counter. They had used the latter as a step and climbed up to the cupboard to get the scissors. I didn't know why such crazed ideas came to fruition in moments like that – when my parenting status completely depended upon the notes taken in a file. The health visitor seemed to just let it go and made some comment about kids' ingenuity and craftiness. I think she could see after spending a little time with them what they were like. There would always be some sort of unbelievable discovery awaiting me. She was probably glad she could go home at the end of the meeting, so she didn't have to deal with it herself.

On another occasion, I had a conversation with her about the prospect of playgroup. I hadn't sent my older daughter to playgroup – she had just gone straight into preschool. I was thinking about putting my younger daughter into it a couple of days a week, but I felt horribly guilty about it. What if she felt like she hadn't had as much quality time as her sister had? What if she couldn't bear the anxiety of being separated from me for the first time? What if I spent the whole morning she was in playgroup beating myself up for having put her there in the first place? I'd even considered the possibility of home-schooling at that stage. (This was pre-COVID, before I'd actually had to do it.) An earlier health visitor had told me about home-schooling groups in the community. She'd made it sound romantic and quaint, so maybe that was the thing that first planted the idea in my head. It was all a far-fetched fantasy, unless perhaps you live on a homestead with acres of land spread around it to send your kids off to. In a small semi in the city, it's a completely different story.

"Do you think I should send her to playg…?" I hadn't even finished the question when she cut me short with a firm "yes." I told her about my feelings of maternal guilt. I had only signed her up for two mornings a week and the health visitor told me that was a mistake. "She's definitely a full-time nursery child – she's more than ready. It will give you freedom too," she said as my daughter proceeded to dismantle the furniture. She made the decision for me, and I was grateful to her for that. I thought I'd really struggle to get through those two mornings a week, but when the playgroup leader offered me an additional two mornings, I jumped at the opportunity like a shark to fresh meat. That was one of those really touching moments in life when your faith in humanity is restored. I'd been having a rough time as a single mum and the lady that ran the playgroup offered my daughter four mornings, but she only charged me for two. She was so kindly that I felt like all wasn't lost. She took a huge weight off me, and I'll always think of her affectionately. She understood how hard single parenthood was without a dad on the scene.

On another occasion, someone put an envelope through the front door. I never found out who did it because the note was anonymous and just read "God bless." It contained £100 and I assumed it must have come from a local church. Sometimes, even when you've lost all faith in people's goodness, you're proven wrong by the acts of strangers. Having children can be extremely difficult at times, but it opens you up to receiving kindness from strangers. You have no choice but to accept help at times. Sometimes it's impossible to even open a door for yourself and if it wasn't for people's kindness at those moments, you'd be completely stuck. It's good to be reminded that you don't just exist as an individual with the power to do everything for yourself. In all likelihood, there will come a time when we are each forced to accept that, so it's better to ready yourself for it early. I'd rather be one of those ladies in the nursing home that accepts help graciously than one of those difficult ones that shows every worker disdain for wiping her bum – not that I'm looking forward to having my bum wiped for me.

There are so many beautiful moments that motherhood brings that you never would have got to experience otherwise. It's what keeps you going during all the strife and the ridiculous moments that you couldn't make up if you tried. Those provide entertainment too, after you've got over your initial annoyance anyway.

I've always liked the idea of a homemade birthday. Maybe I just watch too many YouTube videos where I see people pulling it off on a tight budget. I've never been brave enough to throw a proper party alone, despite the questions that ensued every time we attended another child's party. Or maybe it's nothing to do with bravery and I just don't want to do it.

"Why does so and so get to have the whole class at their party and I don't?"

"Why do they get to go to (insert expensive venue) and we don't?"

"I'm almost ten (says my eight-year old) and I've still never had a big birthday party."

I usually bring up examples to illustrate my point – that they have had birthdays – just not of the thirty kids in attendance kind.

One year, I decided to bake my mum a cake for her birthday. I love baking and experimenting with recipes, but I realised I shouldn't attempt it when someone is waiting for the results. I don't think it's any more economical these days to make one – granted, I did cheat this year and used cake mix and pre-made icing. But I didn't use either of those for my mum. I can take full credit for the mess I made with that one. The pressure was all too much, and I don't perform well under pressure at all – even self-created pressure. If I'm like that when I know a close family member is coming, God knows what I'd be like on the Bake-Off or if I had pursued what I believed to be my life-calling at sixteen (ie, becoming a chef.)

The sponge was like rubber and when I apologised to my mum for the state of it, she just admitted that it didn't taste like cake. She did that thing she does when she's trying hard to detect the fine flavour of a wine and she holds it in her throat for a moment, whilst making her deepest thinking face. I watched her throat pulsing, waiting for a pronouncement, but none came. I could tell she was trying to be polite and to spare my feelings, but her face gave her true feelings away.

I finally got up the courage to try again this summer (with the help of Betty Crocker, but still.) I had visions of how it would look. I decided to stick with buttercream rather than fiddling about with royal icing. It was an unknown and it felt like less would go wrong if I stuck to what I knew. I'm not into intricate detail anyway. I'm more of a "slap it on and hope for the best" type of person, so it just sounded better to me.

I got unicorn and heart sprinkles and pastel writing icing. That was ambitious enough for me. I baked the two layers of the cake and assembled them after letting them cool, of course. (I learned that one the hard way.) Then, I used a knife to smooth the icing around the sponge. It was working out better than anticipated. One big crumb came away with the knife and I had to glue it back on with buttercream. But it looked passable for a kids' birthday party, as long as the parents weren't around and no one inspected it too closely.

I added a lot of sprinkles and then I got out the writing icing. I'd even colour coordinated it with the sprinkles. That was the point at which things really went wrong. It was like whenever a director starts to relax because they've made it to the end of a theatrical production and nothing even minor has gone wrong, and then the whole set collapses around the actors. The writing icing had no pigment in it at all, so it didn't show up with one application. I applied another coat, and another. The writing still wasn't clear. It was just a big wormy blob on top of far too many sprinkles, but it was too late to turn back by then. I covered the monstrosity in a tin foil house and left it to sit overnight, hoping some magic might kick in under its tent when I left the room. Magic and mysticism feel more possible at night, but I can tell you now that none of that came to my aid that evening. I lay in bed afterwards, wondering if I should buy a back-up cake. But there was something charming about the rustic look of it. It was clearly made by my two hands, and it had been made with love, even if it looked like something made by a digestive tract.

The next morning, my boyfriend asked to see it. He usually tells me my cooking is delicious – apart from the time I made Chow Mein, and he feigned fullness to get out of eating it, and the time I made ricotta filled ravioli and spent an extra pound to get the fresh pasta with the luxury filling, and then found out he didn't like ricotta. He probably would have preferred bin scrapings. I knew by his face that the cake didn't look good, and I wasn't just being harshly critical of myself after all. I knew it would probably taste good; it just looked terrible.

"The adults… they will come to the party?" he asked me in his thick Moroccan accent.

"No, just the kids."

"Is OK for the kids. We can turn light out and take it to living room?"

"So, you're embarrassed to be seen with it?" I said, half-laughing, half wanting to cry.

"No, but the adults, they will say things that are not good."

"Like what?"

"To their friends. The adults, they talk to each other, and they will say … we went to house Keelan and we had a cake she made. It did not look good."

So, you admit it looks bad?" I asked.

"No, I just mean for the adults – is ok for the kids."

I was mildly offended, even though I knew that he was just speaking the truth and echoing my own thoughts.

"We'll be turning the lights off when we sing Happy Birthday anyway," I said.

"Will be good," he said.

Anyway, on the day of the party, my daughter had her first "proper" birthday. Only one of her friends was able to come because the rest were away on their summer holidays. I tried to conceal my happiness about that. It was a blessing in disguise, especially because we only have one tiny bathroom. I let her sister invite her friend over too. I hoped the one that had never visited before didn't have high expectations regarding fancy housing, or any experience with custom made cakes for that matter. But kids are always happy to see their friends, whether they see them in a palace or a pigsty.

My daughter's mischievous side came out not long after their arrival. She and her friend had an "accident" in the bathroom with a bottle of hair conditioner. It mysteriously moved position without being touched. It had been emptied and then spread all over the floor. They had thrown all the rolls of toilet roll down the stairs and ruined one by setting it in the body butter. It took longer to clean than anticipated on first glance - and first glance had produced an open-mouthed expression of horror.

I served paper platters of party food, worried as always, that I hadn't made enough to feed everyone. As it turned out, each child ate a single crisp, a cocktail sausage, and a potato ball – and half a bottle of ketchup between them.

Near the end of the party, I unveiled the cake. No one seemed disgusted by it, nor did they seem particularly interested in it. I cut it up after the candles and singing ceremony. None of the kids ate any of it. It was hard to tell whether that was because they'd just had McDonald's and an ice-cream they also hadn't eaten or if it was because the cake was unappealing. I wrapped it up and put it away in their party bags anyway, so it would come back to haunt them later.

My daughter was so pleased with her cake. I was amazed by the look of wonder on her face when she saw it for the first time. I'd never seen her so excited about a cake before. Maybe it was the fact it was covered in little hearts and unicorns, or maybe seeing her name on it was an experience comparable to actors seeing their Hollywood star etched on the ground.

At the end of the day, when we were finally unwinding on the sofa, sitting watching a cartoon before I put the girls to bed for the night, I asked her what her favourite thing about her birthday had been.

She paused for a moment, but she didn't look like she had to take any time to consider what it was.

"My cake," she said proudly. "I loved it."

That was one of those heart-warming moments when you feel like your efforts haven't gone unnoticed. The time I'd put into it and the homely look of it meant more to her than a famous caterpillar cake ever could. I had a slice of the cake. It looked a bit like the cake that Bruce is forced to eat in its entirety in Matilda. I always wanted a piece of that cake - despite the fact he looks ready to reproduce it by the end of the scene. So, we all got a piece of it. It was the kind of cake you have to eat with a fork unless you want to look like you've been bathing in chocolate. It was worth every moment of self-doubt I had in that twenty-four-hour period, and in my parenting to date. Sometimes, when you have to work harder for appreciation, it means so much more to you when you finally get it. That's what I've learnt as a parent. That, and the birthday cake must have been a fluke because I haven't heard an appreciative word about my cooking since.

Chapter Eighteen - One Person's Trash

Today, my kids are at a summer scheme. It's the first one they've been to this summer, and I have the accompanying parental guilt about sending them. Fifty pounds each for two days of freedom. I've always felt bad about paying for childcare. It feels like I'm asking someone to take over my job when I'm technically not in work. If I was a good parent, I think that maybe I should have put the money towards a family day out instead. I should want to spend quality time with my kids every day. I thought that all other parents thought that way until my boyfriend started hanging out with us. He doesn't have kids but being around my kids all the time has produced the same effect of weariness in him. He's an energetic person, but I can see that "I've had enough" look rising inside his eyeballs. When we dropped them off at their workshop yesterday, he jokingly feigned drop kicking them by the bum into the place and then running away.

I used to work on a summer scheme, long before I had kids. I enjoyed doing it, probably because I didn't have my own kids. I could go home to peace at the end of the day and binge watch a TV series in beautiful silence. Now, that's no longer an option, so I guess my patience levels have dropped a little. The laughs make it all worth it though. Yesterday morning, when I was packing my daughter's lunch for the day, I asked her to bring me her school bag. I assumed it was completely empty after the end-of-term clear-out that I actually remembered to do for once, but it had a hefty weight to it; so much so that it was hard to lift it up onto the counter. I was scared to check what was in there. Usually, it's something in a state of decomposition that makes it no longer recognisable. I unzipped the bag.

"Why are there rocks in here?" I asked my daughter.

"Oh," she said, nonchalantly, "those are my babies."

I didn't like to get rid of her babies, so they're still sitting on the kitchen counter, and they'll probably remain there for weeks, or for good. Once someone adds a name to something, or a cute association, I can't bring myself to throw it out. I can't even return these ones to nature like I sometimes do when every bucket is filled to the brim with dry seaweed, pebbles and broken shells. They are destined to remain sitting there, like members of the family. My kids have caught on to this. I think they use it now, as an excuse to keep everything. And they literally keep everything.

My dad is always complaining about the amount of clutter he says my mum has. I'm a clutter bug too. It must be genetic, but my kids are even worse. They can dream up a use for everything, to save it from the bin – or worse – from the charity bag. They hate to think of another child getting to play with their rubbish – even if it was a toothbrush with a head fluffier than mine on a windy day.

My mum gives my kids presents each time they visit her. We always joke with her and send her memes of people visiting their mothers and carrying home enough luggage for a three week stay abroad. Usually, my kids claim ownership of something of hers that is no longer functioning – a single earring without a back, an empty cardboard jewellery box or a loose button. I had a book when I was little. I can't remember what it was called, but I think it was written by Michael Rosen. It was about a kid and his collections. The boy in the book pulled everything out of his pocket. It was all odds and ends, but he treasured those items. I try to remember that book when I'm getting impatient with my kids. All kids love collections – and all kids love to fill every pocket with leaves and twigs and lint that looks like bellybutton fluff. It doesn't make for easy cleaning for their mum, but it's perfectly normal.

I have learnt that if I want to carry out a clear-out, I must do it when the girls are either asleep or out at school. Otherwise, they intervene and make me question my every decision. I'm not good at making quick decisions when it comes to clearing out anyway. My sister is so gifted at it. She just has the innate ability to clear a space in seconds without stopping and having second thoughts. When she came into my kitchen recently, she kindly helped me to clean some of my cupboards. She's radical in her clear-outs. Maybe that's why mine never really go anywhere – they're too half-hearted. I attach meaning to possessions and that's an unwise way to approach them when you're trying to live simply.

Sometimes, I will find the courage somewhere inside me to throw things out before over-thinking. Once they're sealed in the bag, I never remember what's in there anyway. At those times, my kids will inevitably discover the charity shop bag before I've had time to stash it in the car. There have been times when I have thrown out a broken cardboard box and they have fished it out of the bin.

"Why is this in here?" they ask me, accusingly.

"Because it's rubbish," I answer, quietly, putting my head down.

"It isn't rubbish!" they declare in shock. Then they proceed to hug it and pretend that it's their favourite possession.

"It's just cardboard," I say, "It's just rubbish for the recycling bin."

"How dare you call my lovely thing rubbish. It's not!" they yell at me.

I almost start to feel sorry for the trampled packaging. They convince me that it's worth keeping – if not for practical reasons, then for reasons of sentiment.

I used to let them keep the things, but then I realised our home was becoming like a giant skip, so I'd make a fuss of the item and then hide it until they went out of the room. Then I'd deliver it to the bin, praying they wouldn't lift the lid to look before collection day.

I don't ask for their input anymore when we are donating to charity. I'm usually forced to cull our belongings when a birthday or Christmas rolls around. We don't have much storage space left and each celebration has become like every Christmas of my childhood combined. I rarely go overboard with gifts, but other people are generous. Still, each year, it feels like we practically have to pack up a household of toys and give them to charity, just to make room for that year's. My landfill hating heart aches at the thought of the damage we are doing to the environment. But everyone we know seems to be the same. It must be a generational thing. Even the cost-of-living crisis doesn't seem to have tempered it. Kids are entitled and materialistic and that's how society is run, with a few protestors thrown into the mix, waving billboards and conducting marches outside the City Hall.

I try not to dispose of items that mean something to the girls, but sometimes they surprise you with what they remember. They had a house for little figures that I didn't see them play with once, despite the shrieks of glee that had come when they'd first opened it. After a couple of years of neglect, I decided it was time to pass it on to another home. I didn't think the girls would ever notice. They hadn't given it a second glance since removing the packaging. I was trying to dream up a good answer to their question. I knew they already knew the truth, but I didn't want to face the reaction that would come if I admitted to it. I knew they'd see it as a complete betrayal. They'd probably get me to take them in the car to the exact charity shop where I'd deposited it and buy it all back. It's funny because if I'd dared to do that with my parents, I would have been eaten alive. But somehow nowadays, it has become a societal problem that we just bend over backwards to avoid upsetting our kids. Maybe it's because their reactions are so strong, and they have such entitlement about it. Mine talk to me like they're my superiors most of the time, and I thought I was strict compared with other parents my age. But it's just a battle of wills and theirs always seems to win. I do things I would have shaken my head at other parents for doing prior to parenthood. But it's easy to judge when you don't have to deal with it every day, particularly running on no sleep, as I still am most days. I just made so many assumptions before having kids – that they'd be well behaved, that they'd be appreciative, that they'd do what they were told, that they wouldn't be spoilt. I feel like the only thing that would adequately sum it up would be a scowling emoji. Sometimes words just aren't enough. You need to see the facial expression in cartoon yellow to sum it up in modern day terms.

Chapter Nineteen – Snack Menu for Two

My kids are very independent - when they want to be. When they don't, they act like they're confined to the main sofa in the living room, unable to do anything but call my name and list their demands. They only seem to get stuck in that seat when they're watching something that holds their attention – usually an American sitcom that makes the sitcoms of the past look like critically acclaimed filmography. They basically just shout their orders to the kitchen, like I'm running a free restaurant in there. And I can be sure that as soon as I sit down to write or to do anything for myself, they will choose that moment to call my name and ask me to segment an apple or perform a tucking them in on the sofa ceremony.

On so many occasions, after hours of cleaning and feeling the ache in my bones from overwork, I finally sit down in the garden with a cup of warm coffee – a real luxury – and a notebook in which to gather my thoughts. The peace is so beautiful and fresh that you can almost taste it. I raise my cup to my lips and take that first whiff of coffee – it's almost healing. That's the moment when one of my kids will call for assistance in the bathroom or ask to have a cracker and cheese platter presented to them in a specific way, or to have their apple cut up into little cubes, or they'll just start shrieking that they don't have any more underwear and I need to place an immediate order online. That's the moment at which my own mum's toe would have gone up our behinds, had we ever dared to behave like that, which I very much doubt we did.

I can remember behaving well in restaurants. I know everyone sees their own behaviour through rose-tinted spectacles, but ours really was very restrained. We didn't talk much at the dinner table if we were out or if my parents had friends over. We wouldn't have even thought about messing around in public. We didn't want to give our parents a bad name. One hiss of "don't" would be enough to put an end to any noise we made – even if it was only a breath. My kids laugh if I hiss at them. I try to reproduce that pursed lipped look my granny always gave us. I was terrified of it, and I would have done anything to avoid it. I would have done anything to avoid her displeasure – and I did. I listened to Cliff Richard with her, and I didn't once complain. I watched detective programmes and showed a genuine interest in the development of the plot, even when it wasn't exactly age appropriate. I ate up every piece of raw pepper she put into pitta pockets for us without ever grimacing or even wondering whether I liked it or not. It didn't matter whether I liked it or not – I was eating it. I didn't give time to things like considering my likes and dislikes. My likes were whatever adults put in front of me. My kids wouldn't be able to relate to me as a child at all. It's an entirely different existence. They live in the land of entitlement, whereas I lived in the land of "do what you're told or else." They are two places that don't resemble each other in any way. And the strangest part was, overall, I was happy to do what I was told. They're unhappy to hear the mere suggestion of how they should be behaving. And I see all their peers doing the exact same thing.

I struggle to remember a time when my kids said to me. "What do you want to do, Mummy?" "What are we allowed to do?" "Which movie are we watching tonight?" It's all me, me, me when it comes to that stuff. It makes me more selfish in response to it. When I have chocolate in the corner of the kitchen as they're eating a piece of fruit in the living room, I don't feel any desire to share. I do sometimes, but I'd rather just eat it myself. Sometimes it feels like the only thing of your own that you have left.

I remember going out for breakfast once with a group of mums to a soft play café. It was the only one I knew where your kids could play in the next room, supervised while you had something to eat. The lady that worked with the kids was lovely and you could see the play equipment from the café, so it felt like they were safe, and you could really relax while you were there, unless your kids were too young to go in, of course. I had one that was walking, so she was allowed to go in. I could take the baby in if I stayed with her. As soon as she could crawl, she wanted to be in there all the time, so I quickly said goodbye to quiet time. A couple of the ladies I was meeting had anxious kids that didn't want to leave their mums' sides to go and play, so they stayed with us at the table, having tantrums and generally torturing their overtired parents.

One of the ladies got her child a piece of toast with sausage and a carton of juice. After sucking his toast and devouring his sausage, he proceeded to reach for hers. She had a full Ulster fry, but she only had one sausage.

"If you take my sausage, I'm actually going to cry," she said. I was sure I could see tears welling in her eyes as she told him that. I could completely relate to it. Sometimes it feels like your kids have drained every ounce of energy from your body, and they won't leave your side, and in that moment, all you have is that one sausage. If someone tries to take it, you'd consider biting their hand off to prevent them stealing it. Why do kids have a special knack for asking for the exact thing you've been looking forward to? That's the good thing about alcohol and coffee – you don't have to share it with anyone. It's all we have left of "adult world" these days. My mum always talks about how adult and child worlds were separate to one another when I was a kid. There is no line between the two now. My kids are always crossing over the imaginary line and coming onto my side of the globe. Sometimes it's annoying because you waited your whole childhood to finally reach adulthood so you could have adult privileges and now that you've finally earned them, your kids intercept them before you get a chance to enjoy them.

The soft play café closed down not long after that. it was a bit of a greasy spoon, but I was very surprised that it closed. I would have gone there if we'd had to lick the coffee off the grimy floor, just to get a bit of a break. I didn't think places like that could ever close. It was childcare at its cheapest. Maybe the lady that worked with the kids had had enough. She looked about sixty, but maybe she was only twenty at the time – who knows?

Chapter Twenty – Quick Recovery

Having a baby is falsely portrayed by the public and by the media. There are so many hard things about it that no one talks about, or they only mention as a passing comment, like it's not really a big deal. My sister always says she thought it would be like having a cat. We used to have two beautiful Persian cats when we were growing up that sat at the feet of our beds, purring and lovingly snuggling up to us. I don't remember my kids ever lying still like that. I remember my daughter trying to lift her own head up from the day she was born. She was determined from day one. My second became determined as soon as she could reach for a toy.

When my mum first met my second born, she said that she feared for her in the world because she just looked so fragile and scared in those first moments. That was a misconception. She skips into a new place now, filled with hundreds of people, announces her name to the adults like they're her age and she makes a new friend anywhere she goes, even if we're only there for five minutes. Both girls always make friends when they go to the park, or anywhere with other kids. They don't care what age the kids are either. I frequently see them walking hand in hand with kids five years their junior. I think they like to mummy them. Equally, they are never put off by kids much older than them. We were recently in a playground and a couple of teenagers were lying on the big basket swing.

"Can I go and ask them if I can play with them?" my seven-year-old asked me.

"Maybe not this time," I said. "They look about sixteen."

They were taking selfies, probably to send to the boyfriends they would meet that evening in the same park for drinking and general misbehaviour. My daughter wasn't devastated by my turning her down. She just shrugged and did her, " oh well, on to the next thing" face.

Sometimes it's annoying having kids with wills that can't be trampled, when you're trying to get them to properly tidy their rooms or to stop running into traffic, but I guess it will stand them in good stead in the world. Mine aren't daunted by it at all and they just jump into making friends and trying new things. I became a little more like that with age, but I wonder what it's like to have that amount of confidence as a seven-year-old – or even as a baby. The way my daughter scaled those soft play structures at the age of one was like a ninja. I envy that level of dauntlessness at times. I know they're lucky to have that bravery. Maybe when they're grown up, they'll be trendsetting citizens that explore the world independently, inspiring others with their fearlessness. I hope that's what it leads to anyway, and not placements in a teenage detention centre.

That quick recovery thing of theirs crops up all the time. We were recently on holiday and my daughter made a whole new circle of friends in a matter of four days. When it was time to leave the pool for the final time, she howled the whole time we were in the changing room. It's hard to get someone dressed when they're hysterical, but any mum has probably experienced that hundreds of times. I was trying to console her, but I couldn't quite find the words to do it.

"It's sad when you make friends on holiday and then you have to leave them," I said.

I decided it was better to validate her feelings than to try to provide a solution. There isn't a platitude that covers leaving friends, other than making the choice to keep in touch. Sometimes that just feels forced though. People drift in and out of your life and trying to hold onto them is like trying to stop a fish swimming away. It's hard work and it will probably just make one or both of you frustrated in the long run as you're held back from your purpose; you just have to go with life's tides sometimes. It's a hard lesson and one I've never become entirely happy with. Anyway, she was crying and screaming all over the place. Anyone outside the cubicle would have wondered what on Earth was going on in there. Then she gave up on her friends and just started screaming "I want Granda." He was in the changing rooms at the time, but I knew he wouldn't want to see her until he'd finished drying his hair. She doesn't seem to understand whenever it's a bad moment for something. So, I spent the rest of the time in the cubicle trying to contain her and shushing her voice to a more acceptable level. Over pancakes that day at lunchtime, my mum said that my daughter acts devastated about leaving her friends, but the next day, if you mention one of them, her response to their name will just be a blank "who?" I couldn't help laughing because I knew how right she was.

She does have an uncanny ability to attach and then forget anyone in a matter of minutes. I always think she is the definition of a social butterfly. She flutters around, making friends wherever she goes, but she's always moving on to the next thing. I don't know if that's a good thing. I suppose she is more able to accept life's ebbs and flows at the ripe age of seven than I am now in my mid-thirties.

The holiday we went on was amazing in every respect. So many precious memories were made with family and with friends, and my daughter hasn't mentioned her friends once since.

Chapter Twenty-One - Play Date Drama

The plague of the play date begins as soon as you first meet another mum. I like them in measure. Well, actually - no – I like talking to other mums, and I like when our kids happen to get along, which isn't often. It always seems to be the case that if I make a friend of my own, my kids don't take to their children. It feels like they're trying to be wilfully obtuse. Sometimes they make a friend, and even if I like the parents, I think the kid is a bad influence on them. My kids don't need much encouragement to misbehave, but there are some people that are like firelighters to what were just smouldering ashes before they arrived. They bring certain behaviours to the surface and turn bad ideas into bad actions.

I have never felt like our house is ideal for play dates, but there always comes a time when you must reciprocate. Once someone has invited you over for lunch three times, it starts to look very rude if you haven't invited them over once. I always feel like my invitations need to include a disclaimer – mainly because the house I'm living in is practically caving in around us. The wallpaper is peeling off the damp walls, there is visible mould covering most rooms, rainwater pours through the ceiling of the back room when it rains. I'm conscious of the fact that my kids live in an affluent area and everyone we know lives in a better house with an impressive garden space and every amenity they could want at their disposal. When the kids go to their friends' houses, I know they probably live in mansions, or at least something pleasant looking with a nice smell. No matter what I use to scent my home, I can always smell damp. I notice it most when I've been out for the day and come back and my nostrils are assaulted by the stench of it as soon as I open the door. I hope that isn't the first impression that other people have of it too. But scented candles can only cover up so much.

I've started to just invite people over and tell myself that they're there to see us – not the house. But in that area, I would say that is only true twenty per cent of the time. There are plenty of social climbers that are only there to inspect your place of dwelling. I'm aware that I don't know what the real stories of their credit card bills are. I've never owned a credit card, and I think that's probably for the best. But other parents' lives just look much more socially acceptable than mine.

One time, on a playdate, my kids and their friends went to a local ice-cream shop. They always want to go to the place, but I avoid it at any cost because they charge about 20p per sprinkle and the toppings are laid out at kid-eye level and right within their reach. I tell them they can have one sweet, or a couple of smaller toppings. Anyway, the kids were doing that thing they do when they eat with friends. They forget their food, even if they've just said how much they were dying to eat it. Their ice-cream quickly becomes a pool of cream with a few sprinkles thrown in. I encourage them to eat up and they insist they are – but there is always the same amount sitting there. Finally, they were told to gather their cups and to take them with them. They carried them to my house where we planned to continue the playdate.

At the house, they proceeded to dismantle the beds. I had some fairy lights strung up in my daughters' room for decoration. They took them down and wound them around the banister so tightly I had to cut them off and bin them later that afternoon. I didn't find them until after the other kids had left, at which time I was dealing with another emergency. One of the kids had spilt what had become pouring cream with bright flecks in it, and it was all over the kitchen floor. They hadn't bothered to clean it up and I wanted to cry. Accidents happen, but at playdates, it always feels like they happen on purpose. It took a long time to clean the sticky kitchen floor. While I did it, I swore to myself that I'd never host another play date. I did, of course, but I delayed it for quite a while, until my irritation had subsided.

When I was younger, if I ever made a mess, I remember my mum saying to me that I wouldn't like it when I grew up and someone destroyed my house. I wasn't really destroying her house. Ok, there was an incident where my sister and I knocked a bottle of green nail polish all over the new, pale-coloured living room carpet. But other than that, my mum was mostly annoyed if we failed to dust or to dry the dishes and put them away. I remember telling her that I wouldn't care – that it wouldn't bother me if someone made a mess in my house. But something kicks in at the age of thirty and you start to care – even if you didn't before that. I remember as a young adult, when I lived with flatmates, I either had my room very tidy or extremely messy. It was always one extreme or the other. I remember having a friend over once and I couldn't see the floor of my bedroom – and it was a huge room. But now, I'm scared to have anyone over when the place isn't tidy. I clean for playdates, but it's a stupid thing to do because you would need industrial cleaners to come in afterwards anyway, just to make your house liveable again.

Sometimes I think I should have kept the place completely baby proofed beyond the baby years. I didn't realise such daft things would still be happening when my kids were seven and eight. At least they don't try to stick their fingers into sockets anymore, but I caught them eating paper in the car the other day. When I asked them why they did it, they said they were pretending it was chewing gum because the gum had been confiscated after I found it glued to the wall in the landing and disposed of down the back of the sofa.

They don't tend to put little objects into their mouths anymore, which is good, considering the fact every toy they own contains perfect choking-sized pieces. Every time their little cousins come to visit, we have to gather up all their toys and put them out of reach to stop the little ones snacking on them. I don't know what people do when they live with older kids and babies. How do you keep every piece of Lego out of their reach? I find it strange when parents of young kids can just switch off and talk to each other without constantly looking around them. I was always on hyper-alert, and I still felt like there was so many moments of possible danger that cropped up. I can relax a little more now. I know that I can take my eyes off my kids, and they won't always do something dangerous; they just find annoying things to do instead.

Chapter Twenty-Two – Musical Masterpieces

I know that you're supposed to encourage an interest in music in your children from a young age. That's the ideal time to instruct the pupil because they soak everything in that you tell them. Playing becomes second nature. I can remember going to piano lessons at the age of five. My sister must have been three. We went to an old lady's house in our village. She held the lessons at her own piano in her living room. We took it in turns to have our lessons. While one played, the other read all the Beano annuals she'd probably had since her kids were kids. She sat in an armchair in the corner of the room and rapped our knuckles with a ruler when we made a mistake. She whipped the sheet music with the ruler too, to make sure we were following it. I remember learning what middle C was in the first lesson and feeling very proficient and happy I'd gone. If I imagine my kids in a lesson like that now, I don't know how they would deal with it. They'd probably come home and refuse ever to set foot in her house again, declaring her a "mean lady."

My kids have always shown an interest in making music – or just making noise in general. They love playing with Alexa in the living room. They do the kids' daily quiz and play pop songs, singing along at the top of their lungs. Then they get her to fart and burp and laugh hysterically at it. I always wonder if the recordings are of real farts and burps, or if they are just computer generated. Whatever it is, it keeps them entertained for five minutes – which is usually the most you can hope for from my kids.

I bought the girls a toy keyboard years ago. I came across one in the charity shop for £3 and it even had functioning batteries in it. They still regularly play with it, but for some reason, they only tend to play it when they get up for the day, any time between five and seven AM. We live in a semi-detached house, and I remember seeing my neighbour one day. "Have they got a keyboard?" she asked, laughing. I didn't know if she wanted me to answer in the affirmative and then dispose of it, but thankfully she seemed to just find it amusing. She recently vacated the house (surprisingly, not because of us) and we are awaiting the next tenant's arrival. I'm really worried it'll be someone with sensory difficulties, someone that just can't stand noise, or someone that hates being awoken early in the morning. That was me in university. I can remember lying in bed for a mid-afternoon nap and wanting to cry because two kids were bouncing a ball off the wall of the block of flats all day long. Now I'm the mother of those children - although, they aren't allowed to bounce balls on walls. I'm concerned I'll end up next to a business professional type with a serious job – someone with no plans to have a family and nothing but contempt for kids. I have met those types of people, and it is always in those moments that my kids seem to misbehave the most. It's like they can sense they're going to get a rise out of someone before they've even exchanged a word with them.

I was recently pulled aside by their swimming teacher and told that if they didn't stop repeatedly getting out of the pool, they wouldn't be allowed to come back. I was mortified. If I'd done something like that as a kid and had it flagged to my parents, with or without a potential ban, I would have cried about it for years afterwards, every time it popped into my head. But my kids are more resilient than that. Every complaint about them is like water off a duck's back – a duck in an oil slick's back. It's maddening when you're trying to get through to them about something, but I guess it'll serve them well later, when they have to deal with a boss that can never be pleased or someone who shows up under the guise of being a friend, but that really just wants to tear them down.

If anyone annoys my kids, they make sure I know about it. They talk endlessly about people that have caused them trouble. This week, there is a boy in their summer scheme that has been pushing people over, hurting the other kids and he'd admitted to stealing twenty quid from his mum's purse. They were hoping he'd be barred after the first day for his misdemeanours. They told me the leaders had threatened it at the time, but nothing was done in the end. When someone annoys my kids, they seem to struggle to stay away from them. I just advise them to play with someone else and to give the child a wide berth, but they always report back that they've been knocked over or that the kid has stolen their Frube, and binned it before they got a chance to eat it. I never know exactly how they have ended up in the rogue's path again, but they always do – probably sitting right beside them all day long. Sometimes I think they enjoy a bit of drama because it gives them something exciting to discuss afterwards in the car.

I was happy to be with them yesterday, until the fiasco with the swimming class, at least. There are about ten kids in their group, and I can see everything they're doing through the café window. It feels like having a sheet of glass between you should offer you a certain amount of protection for half an hour, but I was summoned by my daughter waving on the other side of the glass. She'd set her inhaler in a puddle next to the pool and the spray mechanism wasn't working anymore. I got it working and returned to the café for the final three minutes of free time.

Watching from the window is usually pretty funny. They're in the first group at the moment. They have divided the kids up into three groups in the one pool. The second group seem to be swimming on their backs and using small floats. The third group are doing the front crawl with their faces in the water. My kids are mostly floating on pool noodles, noodling about. I'm sure they're learning something. If not, it's an expensive conversation with their friends at forty pounds a month. If they get kicked out of the class, at least I'll be a few pounds richer each month, although I'd definitely be poorer in regard to my self-respect as a parent.

Chapter Twenty-Three - Further travels

This week, I went with my kids to a place called Rostrevor. When I opened the visitor information folder in the hotel room, I was panicked for a moment, when I read that breakfast was served from nine o'clock. In our house, breakfast is served at seven on the dot, and that's what my kids think happens elsewhere too. I think I've timed our meals too specifically. I always serve dinner at five. Mainly, it's because if I leave it any later than that, my kids' hunger becomes as unbearable to me as it is to them. Like me, with a little food in them, my kids are much more pleasant to be around. I'm one of those people that is always accidentally early for everything. I think I had it drilled into me as a kid to never be late. It's got to the point now that if I go to my parents' house and they invite me over at 12.15, I pull into their driveway as the clock changes to that time, down to the second. My mum recently asked me if I arrive early and wait round the corner, so I arrive at exactly the right time. I'm just weirdly punctual – unless of course, my kids hold me up – but even then, I have usually factored in extra time. There have been so many times that I've hollered at them to hurry up and that we're going to be terribly late and then we pull up at our destination ten minutes before opening. It's annoying for me, more than for anyone else. It just means I have to wait for everything to start and if I meet someone, I always assume that they'll be punctual too – which they often aren't.

Anyway - back to the breakfast hours at the inn; that village just has a lazier feel to it. It doesn't have that Belfast rush about the place. It feels like everyone takes everything as it comes, and they do what they feel like doing, with regards to housework, leisure or running a business. So, if they don't feel like opening until nine, they don't bother. Thankfully, in small print underneath the breakfast hours, it said that an eight AM breakfast could be arranged upon request, so I headed to reception. I enquired as to whether we could request an earlier breakfast and was met with an immediate, unwavering "no." Maybe the lady was horrified at the short notice of such a request. Thankfully a kindly lady that worked in the restaurant offered to give my kids some small boxes of cereal and digestives with butter for the hotel room to keep them going. They met this offer with great excitement.

While we were in the hotel, the girls got up for the day at 5AM. I thought they might have slept longer with all the walking we'd done the previous day and the fact that we were all sleeping in one room together – but no. They were up at dawn, with the lights on, making huge amounts of noise and eating their breakfast on the floor. They borrowed paper from my diary to play games with and compose lists. They tore it up into smaller pieces, as they always do and ended up scattering them all over the bathroom floor like ugly confetti. They took their Coco Pops into the bathroom, for some unknown reason, and in the process, dropped them all over the floor tiles. They took my boyfriend's phone while we were still half-sleeping and filmed videos of themselves messing around in the bathroom. His phone memory is always filled up and he's picky about what he photographs and films. He gets a storage warning and then realises my kids have pinched his phone again and made a fifteen-minute-long video of themselves dancing in the shower fully dressed or making pig faces into the camera.

After hours of torturing us and probably waking every other guest in the hotel, we finally decided we had to get out. So, at eight AM, on that first morning, we went to the beach. It was a beautiful morning, but even if the rain had been streaming down, we still would have been there. The girls kept asking me for snacks and I tried to hold them off until their second breakfast. We walked along the shore, my grumpiness lifting as we inhaled the sea air. It was really refreshing going for a walk before breakfast; it just wasn't something I ever thought to do. We always ate first and then did everything else after. It was a good way to spend the morning, but it was out of necessity, rather than choice, and I gave a sigh of relief when we got back to the inn and found the restaurant door open. The pancakes were probably the best I've ever eaten – mainly because I was starving, and we'd worked up even more of an appetite with our walk and the exhaustion that comes from constantly announcing the number of minutes left until feeding time to the girls.

The following morning didn't go just as smoothly. There was the usual havoc in the bedroom, but we didn't make it out for a walk to the beach. Maybe we were slowing down to match the pace of the village. But when we went downstairs at 9AM on the dot, the restaurant door was still locked. My heart sank. I couldn't bear the thought of going away and coming back again, especially because we wanted to get on the road again. Thankfully, we heard the door being unlatched from the inside.

"Come in," said the kind lady that gave us the free packs of cereal. We were the only ones there. I wondered if any other kids ever stayed in the inn, and if so, how the parents kept them so quiet and sleeping so late. They must have been a different type of children to mine - or drugged.

For most people, I'm guessing that a breakfast served at 9AM wouldn't be a dealbreaker when choosing a hotel, but for us, it quite possibly could be. Apart from that, our holiday was perfect. I couldn't fault a thing. It might have been nice to have a mini bar in the room though – since I wasn't able to leave the room to go and enjoy myself in the quaint pub downstairs. I just sneaked in tins of West Coast Cooler instead and drank them in the dark after the kids were asleep, like a closet drinker. I hadn't had one of them since I was a teenager, and it was strange, tasting it again, this time on the other side of thirty and with no freedom to stay out all night - but this time, it was because of my parental duties, rather than because of my parents' rules. If only rules worked on my own kids, I thought, as I sipped my expensive lemonade and dreamt up stories I couldn't compose because I was sitting in the dark and I didn't have my laptop. On other occasions like that, I have resorted to writing in the bathroom just so I could use the light without risking waking the girls.

Chapter Twenty-Four - The Fascination with Bathrooms

I feel like we know every toilet in Northern Ireland intimately. Wherever we go, we always quickly get acquainted with the toilet there. I don't know if all kids share this peculiar fascination, but mine love to check out a new toilet – or an old one, for that matter. I can't remember doing the same as a kid, so I don't get the motivation behind their constant trips to what my granny politely called "the Ladies'." There is a pizza place we sometimes visit in my parents' village. Each time we sit down, one of my kids announces their pressing need for a toilet trip. I can understand what motivates them to visit that one slightly more, because the walls are decorated with tiny bird houses, and they have scented hand cream to compliment the hand soap. The place is still freezing, and you literally freeze your bum off when it meets the toilet seat. I always find this to be the case with restaurant toilets. Maybe it's because the windows are always wide open to dispel any unpleasant smells that might interfere with the appetising ones coming from the kitchen.

There is only one toilet I get excited about, and that is the one in the Culloden Hotel. When I visit it, I make sure to pay a visit because it's like a spa in there. They have luxury hand towels, it smells like a beauty salon, and I can use expensive hand creams and soaps that I'd never be able to afford otherwise. The whole experience is a glimpse of relaxation, especially once you have kids and everyone ordinarily follows you into the bathroom or knocks on the door each time you think about having a pee. I like to go to the Culloden to write when I'm on my own and the kids are in school. (Not in the toilet this time.) The hotel feels like somewhere that was made for adults. Usually, I hate places like that. I don't like feeling uneasy when I bring my kids there – and to be fair to them, I have brought the kids there and it wasn't totally unbearable. But it's like a little place of sanctuary reserved for the times when you truly need peace.

Peace is something I never find on any outings with my kids. You can always be sure as soon as we have made it to the front of an exceedingly long queue, they will request to go to the loo. If it isn't at that moment, it is whenever the menus arrive, or whenever I go to put the first forkful of food into my mouth, usually after a half-hour wait for dinner to appear. I get up, begrudgingly, from the table and take them to the toilets. They seem much more excited about that than they do about any other aspect of the meal. I find my kids like the idea of eating out more than they enjoy the actual food. They always ask to go for pizza. We rarely do, but there is a pizza place near us that does a three-course meal deal for kids that's great value. However, it's a bit disheartening when I order it and my younger daughter only eats one quarter of her pizza. The only saving grace is that they like to "come back to it later," so if I remember to get a doggy bag, one or both of the girls will return to it later – usually at the moment I announce "bedtime!" or tell them to go upstairs and brush their teeth. Then they start to rave about the quality of the pizza, and they start planning our next visit there whilst eating it painfully slowly.

Sometimes I wish there was a museum of bathrooms – somewhere a bit like Ikea, but solely composed of lavatories; that would keep my kids entertained for hours. It probably wouldn't have the same effect without running water though. I think that's where ninety percent of the fun lies. I recently left them in the bathroom for a minute, and when I returned, they had made a potion using the two kinds of shower gels I had hanging in the shower. They had added so much water to it that it was no longer useable as soap. I don't know that any of us would have wanted to use a mixture of orange and lavender anyway. Who knows, maybe it'll become a new shower gel craze? Sometimes I wish there was extra high shelving in our bathroom. The fact that there isn't, means that everything needs to be stored on the floor, the edge of the bath or away on a high shelf in my wardrobe that my kids have no hope of reaching. Once it's up there, I can't see it anymore either. There is a stool I use sometimes, but getting it out feels like such an ordeal, and my kids always move it downstairs to use it in their games anyway. Each time I decide to use it, it has been moved to the opposite end of the house and repurposed into a cot for their LOL dolls or they're using it as a chair for their "make-up table." (Make-up smeared bookcase.) I wouldn't have it any other way – but it makes me even less likely to bother looking for whatever is hiding up there.

When I perform an annual clear-out of that shelf, I always find lots of hidden beauty products I'd forgotten I'd even bought. I always tell myself I'll use them soon, but once they go back onto that shelf, they disappear for another year.

Back to the toilet tours – the girls have never got over their fascination with our own bathroom, so I guess it would be expecting too much to think that they'd be able to resist another one with a different lay-out. They love my mum's because it was originally supposed to be a bedroom, but the bathroom was put in there instead, so it's abnormally spacious, with one of those corner baths. It's probably like the soft play area of bathrooms to them. My mum has a lot of bath products too. I've noticed that over the years, more and more of them have disappeared into the cupboard. It must be impractical when we aren't there, but it's probably worth it, to save all the liquids that would otherwise be liberally dispensed into the bathwater.

I've recently noticed that my kids don't write toilets off based on their outward appearance. It doesn't seem to matter whether they visit the ladies' room in a luxury hotel or a dodgy toilet in a forest park with no toilet seats and greaseproof paper instead of toilet roll – they are equally enamoured of both. I'd say that their personal favourite is a port-a-loo; something I would always choose peeing behind a tree over using. They always insist on visiting them, even if it's only for a one second pee. They will claim they're dying to go, just to go in there. I've started holding the door for them on the outside and letting them get on with it. I don't like hovering over a toilet and washing my hands with nothing but hand sanitiser if I don't absolutely have to. We visited some out of necessity recently at a huge picnic in a park. There were hundreds of people there and only a small selection of toilets. Before we approached them, one of the most recent users approached me on her exit from one and said, "they're not for the fainthearted." She was right, but it didn't prevent my kids enjoying their time spent there anyway.

The nicest hotel I ever visited was when I was a teenager. (I could never afford something as nice as that now.) My sister and I shared a room that had classical music playing in the bathroom and a bath that could become a jacuzzi whenever you wanted. It was as deep as a hot tub and that was long before hot tubs became something you ever saw. You can only go downhill from there though – as pleasant as it was – I've had many horrific accommodation experiences since. I think of the bath in that lovely hotel sometimes. It'd probably be all I could afford to stay in if we went there – if only they let out the baths separately from the rest of the rooms. My kids would have a field day in there. They'd probably never make it outside the room to even think about exploring the rest of the hotel, never mind the city.

Thankfully, they haven't done anything too disastrous in anyone else's bathroom yet. They save those little surprises for home. Maybe it's like when a cat lovingly brings a dead mouse specially for its owner and everyone else is spared it.

Chapter Twenty-Five – Stick in the Mud

I decided to introduce the girls to horse riding on a visit to the North Coast last year. They had been on a couple of ponies in a local farm, until that part of the enterprise was shut down. It had only been a twenty feet ride – once across the yard and back. This was something much more ambitious than that. It was inspired by one of those visitor guides left by our Airbnb host – a last minute decision. We drove out to the countryside, to a farm I had never heard of before. It costed more than I expected to, but I've never minded paying for an experience. It's like making use of your rainy-day money. The only problem is that sometimes I haven't had the foresight to save the extra money before the event. Anyway, the girls were given some riding boots and I was sternly warned to wear a pair of them too – even though I wasn't getting onto a horse. I thought that was a little over the top, but I had no idea about the quantities of mud present on a pony trek. The lady told me that the entire walk would take about forty minutes, so the farm was much more expansive than I'd realised.

By the time the ponies got saddled up and they got all the kids sorted out, half an hour had already passed. I thought that would shorten the length of the walk, but I was mistaken. Usually, if you pay for a pony ride, you feel a little cheated by how short it is. We've since experienced a pony ride on the beach and it was over in under five minutes. It did only cost three pounds per child though. This was much more involved than that. There were a couple of adults riding the larger horses, alongside their daughter. They were from Spain, so I didn't know if they understood all the instructions. But maybe horse riding is universally understood. We set off, with me leading my younger daughter's pony. It was like a game of follow the leader, with a lady that worked at the farm at the front of the line. Certain ponies were a bit temperamental and tried to skip ahead in the queue, but they were swiftly put in their place by what felt like a modern version of a farmhand. She reminded me of one of those characters from novels set in the 1800's – someone so countrified that they dress without looking in the mirror and don't mind getting dirt on their hands. They always seem to wear brown, so the mud becomes one with their clothes.

Prior to setting off, they did briefly warn us about the muddiness of the walk, but we spend a lot of time walking in forests, visiting the open farm and going for puddly strolls in the park, so I thought it would be nothing we weren't used to. I seemed to be the only parent leading a pony, but the rest of the kids looked slightly older than my youngest. Some of them were experienced horse riders. You could tell they came there all the time. They had those local Scottish tinged accents they seem to have in that area and they were just so confident in what they were doing.

I used to do horse riding as a kid. I didn't stay long enough to progress beyond a pony or to do galloping and things like that, but I loved what I did learn. I wanted my kids to experience that feeling too. There's something about it that just switches everything else around you off – you are in deep concentration, and everything becomes still. But my kids must be a different variety of children because they were jabbering away on the backs of the ponies, asking four thousand questions a minute. As I ploughed on, trying to disengage my boots from the swamp we were walking through, they asked me about the ponies' names, the ponies' feeding habits, the ponies' life histories. My kids always think I know the answer to everything, and although that is flattering, it definitely isn't true. In fact, sometimes I have to ask them questions to find the right answers. There is a lady that set up a style site with her daughter online. They make videos of people removing their clothes as they reveal personal truths. I know this sounds like an inappropriate link to make to a children's activity but bear with me. I remember her talking about her relationship with her daughter and the fact that they set up their business together. "Our children are our greatest teachers," she said. And it's true – I have learnt so many life lessons from mine, I have learnt so much about myself from them (quite a few things I could have done without knowing, but still,) and I have learnt so much about my own limits. As it turns out, one of them is leading a horse through a swamp whilst trying to keep up with a barrage of questions. It turned out the trek was good value for money – it went on for a long time. I wondered if I paid extra, could I make it end sooner? I could feel mud everywhere. My boots were like two chocolate cake whisks and my legs and torso felt damp too. The pony kept (just) missing my feet. I didn't know how people made leading a horse look so effortless. I guess they didn't have a six-year-old on its back demanding to know the answer to every question in the world at the same time.

When we got back, we had to go into a barn and get the horses to perform beginner's tricks. I was ready to hit the road by then, but everyone on horseback was still having fun. At least I could watch it all from a safe distance by then. After everyone had cantered around the barn, it was finally time to hit the road. The first thing my younger daughter said to me upon dismounting the pony was that I had mud on my back. My legs were coated in mud, my coat was coated in mud; the addition of the riding boots had been purely academic.

"You have mud on your bum, Mummy," my kids laughed in delight.

We happened to be staying on a farm in a little cottage, so at least it was a fitting environment for my ensemble. Although, inside the holiday cottage, everything was immaculate. I knew I'd have to strip off at the door and have a shower as soon as I returned. My clothes didn't have to be binned, but they had to be washed in the place. I don't think I've ever really done laundry on holiday before. I just brought enough outfits to last, or I used some travel wash in the sink and hung them up to dry in the heat. But that was abroad. In Northern Ireland, there is no heat, and for that mess, travel wash wouldn't have cut it.

Hopefully, if I take my kids horse riding again, my youngest will have reached the age threshold for unsupervised pony rides. I might even get a horse for myself. If I was elevated, I'd be much less likely to get sucked into the swamp. My kids still talk fondly of that experience, and they still tell everyone that I had mud on my bum. I guess I could have had worse on it. Maybe I did and I was none the wiser.

Chapter Twenty-Six - Climbing Uphill

I've developed a bit of an obsession with climbing high hills. I'd love to go hiking in the mountains, despite my asthma, but I don't know if my kids would go along with it. Someone told me they recently went wild camping in the mountains. I like the idea of such an endeavour, but I'm also not outdoorsy enough to pull it off. I don't mind getting caught out in the rain, or going for a long walk on uneven terrain, but I like to be able to have a warm shower and a cup of coffee somewhere with central heating afterwards. Maybe if I knew how to make a campfire, that would suffice. But I'm worried if I try, it'll either smoulder away to nothing, or that I'll be one of those people that starts a forest fire that destroys all the natural beauty and animal habitats for miles around. I don't want to appear on the news for that.

Anyway, I find it really freeing walking to the tip of a hill. I've only been to the top of a mountain once, and that was as a kid. We got stuck at the top in a thunderstorm, so it didn't really inspire me to set out on more mountain hikes – majestic though the lightning bolts were. I have a feeling my kids wouldn't be up for that anyway.

There must be a lot of pit stops when people set off on a hike with kids in tow. That, or they've been trained to walk uphill since birth, probably strapped to the back of their hiker parent. I don't really know what I'm doing, and sometimes I wonder if it's safe to try, without another adult there to supervise.

One day, I decided I just had to go to the top of the Cave Hill. I'd been watching it from below since I was a kid, and I wanted to see it from another perspective. I'd been told there were trails on it and it was a fairly straight-forward walk – apart from some poor signpost markings. That would have been my downfall. We probably would have ended up stranded there, like more sensible people end up stranded in the real wilderness – not even a mile away from the nearest police station. I decided not to chance it until I'd familiarised myself with the route. We drove to the upper car park and walked from there. It was only a twenty-minute walk from there to the top, and only the end part was slightly steep. When we were walking up the stony pathed part that led to the much-anticipated view, my daughter tripped and fell. She cut her knee. It was nothing serious, but it was enough to put her off the place. If something happens to my daughter in a place, she blacklists it, even if said occurrence is brushing against a tree branch without causing an injury. She'll swear that she's never setting foot there again, which is inconvenient for me when I really want to return somewhere. It always seems to happen at the places I most want to revisit too. After her fall, I hoped there wouldn't be any other disasters. I knew on a hilltop; it could have been a lot worse. At least they'd got to poke in a stream and enjoy looking at the birds before disaster befell her.

When we got to the top, I had a bit of a surreal experience. There was all of Belfast lying beneath us – tiny and like a view from a plane, and there on the top of the hill, sat a couple I knew, having a picnic. There weren't many other people around, so it was weird that we happened to bump into them right there. It confirmed my pronouncement that Northern Ireland is so small you run into people from the school run wherever you go. There is nowhere to run to. At least they were an affable couple I enjoyed talking to. It could have also ended up being much more unfortunate than that. The girls and I planted ourselves on a patch of grass. My daughter was leaping around, and I was repeatedly shouting at her to sit down. I was waiting for her to try to throw herself off the hilltop. We sat down and had some hot dogs I'd brought in a flask. I thought it was all very romantic and memorable, but my daughter was not a fan of the view.

"It's too high," she squealed. "I don't like it."

"Can you finish your hotdog first?" I pleaded. "Come further away from the edge so you can't see as much."

She was happy to move, but it didn't put a stop to her complaints. We rushed our hotdogs, and I took a few photos as evidence that we'd made it there – even though our car had done most of the hike for us. The views were so clear that day and spectacular. I wanted to sit for ages, poring over them and identifying each landmark that lay beneath us. But there wasn't time for that. We gathered our stuff and started the descent back to the car. My daughter was still expressing her loud displeasure about being there. We passed a few dog-walking couples making the upwards walk. They all looked blissfully happy. My daughter was continually making a noise like a displeased parrot. It didn't really go with the peaceful backdrop.

I'm sure there were lots of singing birds to hear and mooing cows. I'd even spotted some that resided on the hillside. I pointed them out to my daughter, to distract her. But I got the feeling that nothing short of a birthday parade would be enough to distract her. Do you ever get the feeling, if you have kids, that they behave that way when you have chosen the destination? Sometimes I wonder if it's genuine ill-ease, or if they just don't like the fact that there's no playground and their legs might get a bit tired. They don't like that they aren't in control of the day out.

A long twenty minutes later, we made it back to the car. My daughter was labelling the whole experience "scary" and declaring that she "never wanted to go again." My younger daughter, who had seemed happy enough until her sister's complaints got into her head, was nodding sympathetically, and patting her sister on the shoulder. "It's over now – we're going home," she said. She's good at comforting her when she needs to be detached from the emotional climbing wall she's stuck on. I felt pretty low about the whole day out. I wished we had just stayed at home and that we hadn't gone on an adventure after all. That's the problem with kids – they're brutally honest when they don't like something, so you'll never have to sit and wonder whether it was all they hoped it would be. And it usually isn't. My kids always end up getting most excited by an urban park with no wildlife to be seen in it, metal, chipped paint, rusted bars, and a broken slide. They never seem to be able to fully appreciate when you take them somewhere special. They just want something to climb and play on, however ugly and unhygienic that thing might look.

For some reason, whenever I make a trip like this, it's like I get amnesia about how it unfolded the last time. I have been back up the Cave Hill since, but I did it when the girls were in school. But whenever the location changes, even if it somewhat resembles aspects of the last disastrous trip, I forget and assume they will be delighted to visit the new place.

Yesterday, we had a funny excursion. It started with a trip on a steam train. I could picture it in my mind before we arrived there. It would be like a scene from The Railway Children – an adventure that they would talk about for years to come. We were in a hurry that day. For once, I hadn't allowed enough time to get there, and I wasn't entirely sure where the place even was. The directions provided online were vague, and made it sound like the train's destination was a railway museum and café. It said the trains ran every twenty minutes, so I thought, perhaps it would be twenty minutes long. But I was sure it would be a memorable twenty minutes, nonetheless.

We raced onto the train. The ticket inspector waved my phone away when I tried to open the tickets. I thought that was very generous of him - and trusting – he didn't know if we had pre-paid. The girls excitedly climbed on board. There was whistle blowing and "choo choo" noises, which the girls didn't seem to take under their notice. We got a compartment to ourselves and took our seats. The girls played with the armrests for five minutes while we waited to go, and they got out of their seats tens of times, while I repeatedly told them to sit down. Why do even short waits feel long with energetic kids? I always see kids, everywhere we go, sitting sweetly next to their parents. Sometimes it's in a takeaway, a cinema screening, or in a doctor's surgery. But mine don't do that. They're always on the move and I'm always hollering at them to come back. Anyway, with bums finally planted on seats, we set off.

"We're moving," shrieked my daughter. "Where are we going to?"

"You'll have to wait and see," I said.

I always hated when my parents said that to me. I didn't particularly want to be surprised and I wanted to know what they knew before we arrived at our destination. Now I know that it isn't because parents hold some sort of privileged information and they want you to perpetually be in a state of surprise – it's because they can't be bothered answering, haven't made the decision themselves yet, or most commonly, because their heads are spinning so much from living with kids that trying to come up with a pleasing answer would be close to impossible. So, long story short – I say it all the time now too.

"Oh, there's our car," shouted my daughter as we passed the carpark.

It wasn't clear where we were going to and there were no announcements, just whistle blows – but that was part of the fun. We arrived at a second station a minute later. I thought it was to let more people aboard, but I guess it was just part of the route. I was surprised when we changed direction and went back towards our starting point.

"There's our car!" shouted the girls.

"What's happening?" asked my daughter, making a face.

"I don't know."

"Is this it?"

"I'm sure it's not," I said.

It had been surprisingly cheap compared to most other excursions of its kind (five pounds each per ticket) and I'd thought it was great value for an experience like that.

We got to the original station, and I got ready to set off in the opposite direction. We must have just been picking up a few stray passengers before we set off. But the whistle blew. I didn't know if that meant we were supposed to get off, but no one shooed us, so we just stayed put. The ticket inspector was waving in a friendly manner from the platform. I guessed that meant we hadn't done anything wrong. It's hard to know what the rules are when you've never visited somewhere before. Especially when there was no one to ask on the train. We set off again – in the same direction as the first time.

"Oh, there's our car again!" yelled the kids. Their excitement at spotting it never seemed to wane. It was probably what a celebrity sighting felt like for anyone else.

"Is this all it is?" my daughter asked.

"I don't know," I said. I looked out the window, trying to figure out what was going on. Maybe there was some technical difficulty occurring that I had no idea about. But no one looked alarmed. The staff all seemed happier than most of the fellow tourists I've ever met on holiday do when they weren't even working. The train went to what I'd thought was an extra stop and then back again.

"There's our car!" laughed the girls.

"If this is all it is, it's ridiculous," my daughter declared.

I shushed her and warned her to be polite. She was just voicing my own thoughts, but I still didn't want anyone to overhear them.

When we arrived back at the first station one minute later, I got to my feet. "Maybe that's it and we were already meant to get off," I said.

We walked into the gangway, and I ran into one of the members of staff, dressed in his traditional train inspector outfit. At least the costumes were on point.

"I don't know if this is a stupid question," I said. "But when are we supposed to get off?"

"Now!" he shouted, cheerily. "I'll help you with the door."

I'd never met someone before who was so kindly about kicking us out. We got to the door, and he started to pull it open when someone told him off with a hand gesture and one of their staff's signature smiles.

"I'm going to get in trouble now," he smiled. "Oh, you don't get off yet – you get one more go."

It felt more like we were in an amusements arcade with a faulty machine than on a life-altering steam train experience in that moment.

We returned to our compartment, which was lovely. It had red seats with leather armrests that could be raised or lowered. There was a wide window that gave us a good, clear view of our car. It would have been a luxury train ride had we been allowed to stay on it for longer than ten minutes.

I didn't bother taking my backpack off my back. It felt pointless when we'd be getting off after one more turn. The girls were looking out the window in disbelief. Even they were seeing the laughable irony of the fact that they had said "there's our car" about twenty times. We had all mistakenly thought we were going on a day long adventure and that we wouldn't see our car until we returned after the long trip ended. I'd thought it's yellow colour would have become dulled in my memory by then, but it was as vivid as ever.

We disembarked the train and learned that a herd of newcomers were waiting to get onboard. For how remote the place was, it was surprising that so many people seemed to visit it. There was a stall on the platform that sold kids' train themed colouring books, teddies and knick-knacks. It was great value for a museum shop. There were even items for 30p, but I couldn't get any of them because it was cash only and the cash in my purse came to a grand total of 7p. It's problematic as a parent to never have loose change. Between collections sent out by the school, shopping centre rides and buying odds and ends in shops that haven't yet heard of

Mastercard (or tax fraud), it is always required, and yet, I never seem to have it.

"Sorry," I said, "You won't be getting anything like that today."

They didn't act surprised. "You always say no," is their most used pronouncement in shops.

We called in to the platform café. More than anything else, it was just to drag the experience out a bit. I hadn't spent the extra money to enter the train museum, but from what I could see, it looked like it was more of a train room – not unlike the compartment in which we'd just spent a valuable fifteen minutes (at a push.) We got a snack and a drink each and sat in the highly polished room. I liked it – it was like a cross between the Ulster Transport Museum and the Titanic Hotel. We sat next to the empty fireplace and the girls found glass jars filled with more memorabilia for 10p. I didn't even have 10p, but it didn't stop them sticking their hands in the jars repeatedly anyway. Sometimes I think kids like to touch things tens of times when they can't get them to somehow convince themselves that they've owned them for a moment. I felt bad that I didn't have the change to get them a Thomas the Tank Engine flag each. But not bad enough to get up from the table, walk across the café, join the queue, and plead to make a card payment.

When we were finished, we went to the playground next to the carpark. That was a bigger hit than the train had been, and it was, of course, free of charge. Sometimes I fall into thinking that kids want scheduled outings, when really, they just want to mess around in the park, get a packet of sweets and make some friends they'll never see again. They always seem happiest when they're doing those simple things. The playground had a climbing wall and a climbing frame shaped like a climbing rock. They loved it so much that it was hard to peel them away from it. They did make the obligatory trip to the toilet, and that park toilet was not pretty. Even the girls commented on how horrible it was, so it must have been truly filthy. We didn't make a second visit anyway. It feels like that should go down in a book somewhere because it truly was record-breaking.

After that, I took them to visit a lighthouse I walked to when they were in school last year. It was on a cliff top, and the views were stunning. This is where the connection between this place and the Cave Hill begins. I didn't think of the heights-aspect. Before that, we had our picnic in the car. It was spitting outside, so I decided to let it dry up first. The girls were already looking a little tired, but from what I remembered, the entire walk there and back took about twenty minutes. They were cheered by their salami sandwiches. Each time I think I've thrown together a boring lunch, it ends up being the one they love the most. They made so many crumbs in the backseat that I didn't know how they'd actually tasted the bread, but it just added to the pre-existing mess on the floor anyway.

Which sends me off on a momentary tangent. Each month I get my kids to clear the mess out of the car. They have to throw out the rubbish, hoover and put their toys back into the house. It is never an easy undertaking. The weird thing is, no matter how long it takes, and how many melted lollies they have to unglue from the floor mats, they seem to suffer amnesia about how long it took to clean it. The same behaviour resumes that same afternoon in the car. It seems that they'd rather live messily and have to deal with the consequences of it than to pick up as they go and have less to do. That always surprises me. I thought their laziness would make them a little savvier than that.

Anyway, back to the lighthouse. After they made breadcrumbs all over the car, we began our walk. They were asking if there was a playground before we even made it to the coastal path, and it was only a few feet from the carpark. I considered taking them to the bathroom, but I was worried we'd find worse there than we did in the last one. There were only a handful of other people walking there. I liked how tranquil it was, apart from the whining, of course.

My kids aren't bad walkers, but when they're in the wrong mood, it can be a recipe for disaster – especially if they've been fighting with each other before they've got out of the car. I realised that eating in the car had been a mistake – it left their mouths and hands empty on the walk. Maybe if we'd walked while we ate, there would have been fewer complaints. Still, it was too late to do anything about that by then.

The lighthouse looked deceptively close to us, but the more we walked, the further away I realised it must have been. Walks on your own are completely different to walks with kids. If you manage to complete a pleasant walk in fifteen minutes, it's not because the walk is inherently easy – it's because your kids aren't with you. That's something I always remember while I'm walking with my kids, but that I fail to remember as soon as the walk is over, and the complaints have relented.

There weren't many other people around, even though the carpark was filled with camper vans. A tent was pitched on the grass but there was no sign of the campers. They must have been sleeping inside, I thought – or off on a trek. Halfway to the lighthouse, the rain started. Thankfully, we had all brought raincoats. Another family dashed past us, telling us they didn't have any coats. I didn't even have an umbrella to offer them. The lady said we were ready for the outdoors. I've never had anyone say that to me before. It was nice to think I was prepared for once. I didn't think of myself as having any sort of outdoor survival skills. Granted, putting on a raincoat isn't like using a fishing rod or an ability to make a fire pit, but it was better than nothing.

We stood under a shelter that resembled an ancient bus stop. We were crammed in with three other families. None of them moved in to make room for us, so we just hung out where the roof pooled water onto the ground for a few minutes and then decided to walk on. Then, I didn't see a soul for ages. Finally, we arrived at the caves. I must have over-stated how exciting they were to the kids because they immediately expressed their disappointment with them. There were some guys with their fishing equipment, but even they were standing pressed back against the cave wall, sheltering from the weather. As we walked around the cliff edge, one of my daughters tried to skip off while the other one gripped my hand like I'd only ever seen her cling to a present she didn't want to pass on in a game of Pass the Parcel. It felt like we'd gone to such great lengths to get there, that it would have been a waste to leave without seeing the lighthouse. So, we climbed the steps that wound around the cliff edge, my daughter whinging at me the whole time and me shouting at my other dare devil daughter to stop trying to escape my grip. We reached the pinnacle, and the lighthouse was revealed. The last day I had been there, the weather had been much fairer, and the views were spectacular. That day, they were obscured by the clouds in the skies. My kids expressed their disinterest in the lighthouse, so we turned back to make our long descent to the carpark. On the way back, it was still raining, but it was no longer a deluge. Still, the two fishermen remained sheltered under the part of the cliff that jutted out. They spoke to us as we passed them.

"Is it like that the whole way up?"

"Yeah, I think we picked the worst day ever for it," I laughed.

"We came camping here because we thought the weather was meant to be good."

"Yeah, the weather forecast lies – it's always the opposite to what they say it will be," I replied.

I've often considered seeking a job in that area, for that specific reason. Someone must be getting paid to look out the window and still get the forecast wrong as it's happening ninety per cent of the time. A job with no skill required – that sounds like my kind of gig.

The two guys didn't look like they had plans to fish any time soon, which made me wonder if they were regular fishers or if they had just run with an idea they had for the weekend. Maybe it was just a reflection on us and how crazed I was to consider an outing in such weather.

Finally, after what felt like hours of complaints, we got back to the car. I'd never been so happy to see my yellow sunbeam of a car before – even though the inside of it resembles a skip and I have to endure radio songs I'd rather pull eyelashes out than listen to, just to keep my kids' fights to a minimum.

I knew we needed a reward, more than ever before. And I'm big on rewards; mainly for myself, if I'm being honest. So, we drove to a town that my granny lived close to when I was little, and I took the girls to an ice-cream shop where I had spent many happy Saturdays in my childhood. I was weird how little the place had changed in thirty years. The videos they used to rent out were long gone, but they still had their specialty chocolates counter and the weird coasters I'd never seen anywhere since. They were a bit like the napkins that old ladies used when they were having tea served from a tea trolley – little doilies with words printed onto them. We had our ice-creams, and my kids expressed their disappointment about the fact that they were only allowed a small cone each. When I was a kid, that was the ice-cream I got every time. I still remember being promoted to a medium cone around the age of ten and thinking that was a really big deal – like it was the first marker of adulthood. Recently, when we were on holiday, I allowed them to get the cones they're usually never allowed to have. They were huge waffle ones dipped in some sort of blue sherbet that encircled the top of the cone. I wouldn't even have dared to ask for one when I was a kid, or taken it under my notice as a possibility, but that's one of the big differences between my generation and my kids' generation. They feel comfortable asking for the biggest cone. Even if they're turned down multiple times, it doesn't make them lose hope. They keep asking until they wear you down and you agree to something you never would have offered in the first place, had they left the decision to you. I just hoped their eyes weren't bigger than their bellies.

There's nothing I hate more than food waste, which is an issue I'm faced with daily. I always end up scraping three quarters of their dinner into the bin. We could feed a small country on their unfinished meals, and that makes me really sad. Maybe I'm just a "gorb" because I never leave a crumb on my plate. Even as a kid, I ate almost everything. I only drew the line at the fat on meat and my dad's parboiled potatoes. He was never patient enough to wait for them to cook. I can still hear my mum saying, "there's a bite to them," but he never seemed to notice it. He was always a fast eater, and she was a slow one, so maybe he didn't have time to notice in the second the potato spent in his mouth between plate and stomach. Anyway, my point is – I ate practically anything, even if I wasn't fond of it. But my kids throw away food they genuinely like, just because they can't be bothered finishing it.

Both girls ate their ice-creams reasonably quickly on the day of the big blue cones. But neither of them touched the cones. It was ridiculous, considering the fact they had specifically chosen those ice-creams for the cones, and they hadn't even tasted them. But if there's one thing I've learnt about my kids, coercion doesn't work when I'm trying to get them to eat something. I couldn't even eat them because the cones were filled with dairy ice-cream and that doesn't agree with me, if you know what I mean. So, I permitted them to put the cones in the bin. I could hear my mum in my head saying, "that's a sin." And I had to agree – it really felt like it was. I'd thought they'd dreamt of those cones for years, waiting for the day when I might finally say yes to one. But the day had arrived, and they didn't care about them – they were prepared to just toss them away without a second thought.

"I can't believe you asked for those and didn't eat them," I said. I felt like I had to play the role of the nagging mother, even though I knew it would have no real impact on them. They just don't feel bad about things in the same way I did as a kid. I cried over nothing, including the feelings of inanimate objects. But they are so flippant about things – it was pointless trying to bring them around to my way of thinking. We are just differently wired. Maybe their wiring makes them more resilient, so it's no bad thing – except where expensive ice-cream is concerned.

I swore I wasn't going to buy them another ice-cream on that holiday, but I did. But I only allowed them to get a teddy cone each time with one scoop of ice-cream. They didn't even argue about that because they knew they weren't capable of eating the large cones from first-hand experience. People always say that's the best teacher, and I guess it is. It definitely works better than my nagging and shouting do anyway.

Does anyone ever wonder what the neighbours would say about the noise levels coming from their houses, if politeness wasn't a factor? I know our house must sound like there are chimpanzees loose in it most days. And there are. The creatures that live there create the same levels of destruction anyway. Sometimes, people act alarmed when they witness one of my kids' tantrums – and their age doesn't seem to have eased them any.

I remember one day recently I took the girls to a family day that was on at a local outdoor venue. They had lots of free activities for kids, but mine just weren't in the mood for them at that moment. Maybe they were over-tired, but they were acting like everything was completely boring. That always makes me want to subject them to the true meaning of boredom, to teach them a thing or two. I always think back to myself as a kid and how gracious and appreciative I was of everything. At least, that's how I remember it. Like my sister said to my mum this week – why were we such perfect children?! I guess everyone thinks that when they look back on something they are well distanced from. But I think we were reasonably well behaved. Apart from one occasion, when I cut my sister's fringe for her and left little hedgehog style spikes on top of her head, I can't think of much that we did wrong. She said she was happy with the haircut anyway. But I've probably just conveniently forgotten all the moments of frustration I caused. I'm getting payback now – that's for sure, but I just tell myself it will help my kids out later in life. They won't be daunted by anything, and they will venture out into the world without letting any reservations eat away at them.

I really admire my kids' confidence. In fact, I wish I'd had a tenth of the confidence they have when I was a kid – or an adult, for that matter. I remember making myself physically ill with worry over things like a book review I had to present to the class. This year, my daughter had to do a presentation on Iceland in front of the class, and it didn't seem to faze her. There were thirty listeners in the room, but she didn't seem to get overly anxious about it. She just went with the flow. That was something I never did. They're always showing me the ways in which I could have been different. It might be too late to correct it now, but it puts things in perspective, and I see just how much I caused myself heart failure over things that didn't deserve a moment's worry.

You're never too old to learn something you could have done differently. It makes you view your own experience through a different lens, and it makes you rethink your behaviour as an adult too. You don't just teach your kids things; I think they teach you far more than you could ever imagine. Every week, when I watch them through the café window at swimming lessons, I see how much I missed out on just by being a worrier and an overthinker. They make a new friend a minute. There doesn't even seem to be a period of introduction or getting to know each other; they just act like they've always been a part of each other's lives. I love how accepting they are of people. But they are also reasonably accepting of the fact that life is ever-changing and moving and that just because they've made a best friend in the park, it doesn't necessarily mean they'll ever see them again. And they usually don't mind that – they're able to enjoy it for what it is, and continue through life, making new friends and saying hello and goodbye, often on the same day. It's taken me my whole life to understand that. I used to think everything had to have a deep meaning – that if you had a great conversation with someone in the park, it meant that you should try to develop and sustain that friendship. But some things are just for the moment, or to brighten each other's lives that day and then move on. They've learnt that so much sooner than I have. Or maybe it just comes naturally to them – some sort of coding in their DNA that I'm lacking but that would have made things far easier for me.

Were you one of those confident kids in school that everything seemed to come easily to? Or was everything a struggle? I would say that more people from my generation belonged to the second group. But most kids I meet nowadays have such confidence and self-belief. It's both inspiring and mystifying. Maybe they've just always been encouraged to speak up and let their opinions be heard. We weren't asked our opinions, and if we had the cheek to give them, they were promptly squashed. Maybe that's where the difference lies. But I also remember just being afraid of adults as a kid. I didn't want to displease them, and I didn't want to get in trouble. Mine just seem to view adults as friends – like each one is a big sister or brother that they can have fun with. And if they do encounter a rude or unpleasant one, it doesn't bother them for long. They just talk about how "mean" or "rude" the adult was. They'd probably gladly give them a dressing down if the opportunity presented itself. It seems like the parents do more to tiptoe around their kids these days than the other way round. I don't think I've ever seen my kids worry about an adult's mood, or the fact they've upset them, or the fact that the adult is sick and incapacitated. It's all just about the fact that the adult isn't meeting the demands at their usual rate. What really stands out to me is the time when I was running up and down the stairs to meet their bedtime demands and I fell on the stairs. Whatever way I fell really hurt, and I lay there winded for a while. It was the kind of injury where you can't speak for a few minutes. I don't know if the girls heard the fall, but they didn't rush to my aid if they did.

"Mummy, where's my water?" one called.

"What's taking so long?"

Those types of comments send me straight into parental indignance. I just can't believe the audacity of them, and I find it hard not to draw parallels between that kind of behaviour and my own childhood. I wouldn't ever have dared to say something so rude. So, I expect them to know that it's appalling too. But they don't seem to view it that way, however I present it to them.

"Mummy, why aren't you answering?" they shouted.

It was the only time I can ever recall them not getting out of bed – and I hadn't even told them not to get out of bed that time. I prefer that they don't see me wounded though. It's like catching you in a weakened position and I always worry they'll take advantage of that. I don't want them to see me fall either. But I'm not against crying in front of my kids. I always think that if you hide every tear, what does it teach them about expressing emotion? Does it teach them to suppress their own feelings? I'd rather my kids know it's ok to have a good cry – sometimes it's the only remedy you need. Keeping stuff like that inside can't be healthy. One time, I tripped over my daughter's bike in the back garden and fell on the concrete. I was at my heaviest then, so I came down pretty hard. Falling as an adult is entirely different to falling as a kid. You don't bounce up again. I cut my knees and I was sitting on the sofa, crying like a toddler with, well, a grazed knee. My kids consoled me and even put a Minions plaster on my knee. Sometimes they end up mummying you when you didn't even see it coming. Thankfully, I haven't had many major injuries since being a mum. That would make me incredibly stressed. I feel sorry for mums that end up being hospitalised and they can't bring their kids with them. Although, once they sort out the practicalities of childcare, maybe it just feels like a bit of a holiday. I know I would hate it though – I hate being incapacitated. I plan to be like my granny, who kept shopping long after she stopped being able to walk. That steely determination made her drive over strangers' feet in her Shop Mobility scooter to get to the clothing racks and she didn't even pause to notice their annoyed looks.

There are times when you'd gladly swap places and take your kids' suffering from them though. Not long ago, my daughter got a tummy bug. I didn't see it coming. We rarely do – apart from in one example I'll elaborate on in a moment. Why do tummy bugs only ever strike in the middle of the night? Or when you're in the car? I don't think we've ever had one that conveniently began in the bathroom. Anyway, my daughter sleeps in the top bunk and later that night, I heard her calling me.

"Mummy, I threw up."

I immediately assumed she'd been sick in her bed. I dread that. Changing sheets in a bunk bed and disinfecting everything whilst trying not to wake their sister is always difficult beyond description. But this was something else entirely. Excuse the unwanted detail, but she had thrown up from the top bunk all over the room. By the time I reached her, she was about to go again, and I decided I might as well let her finish what she started there because it couldn't get much worse. At least then, it was contained in one room. On that occasion, I had all the lights on and all the cleaning products out. My boyfriend brought me gloves and a whole new pack of cloths. I nearly used all of them. It's something I hope to never relive. It does seem like a once in a lifetime kind of experience, but with my kids, you never know. My daughter seemed to make a miraculous recovery immediately after projectile vomiting to a degree I had gladly never seen before. She provided a running commentary of the clean-up as I performed it and she and her sister watched the whole disaster from the doorway. It almost became a bragging right for her. "I threw up from the top bunk and it went all over the room."

It even covered her library books that we had just taken out that week. Thankfully, most of them had plastic covers that were able to take a lot of disinfectant without tearing apart. I guess that's why those covers are there. Or maybe the librarians never could have anticipated something of that scale happening. I supposed books probably got dropped in the bath now and again, or sucked by a baby, but I wondered how many copies had been through the same ordeal as ours. It slightly put me off the idea of sharing books with the rest of the community for a while. However well you cleaned them afterwards, they'd carry that history with them. The next reader would never know, but I would always know. It opened up so many horrible possibilities in my mind of what could have happened to the books you had just borrowed. Gross.

Chapter Twenty-Seven – Blank Baby Books

There are so many precious moments spent with kids, you wish you could catalogue all of them. But if you did, it would be so time consuming that you'd miss out on the actual moments as they occur. That's how I feel about baby books. That's how I justify not having religiously filled them out to myself. Before having my first born, I shopped around for the best baby book. My ex-husband told me to make sure I got one that covered the first five years, and not just the first five months. It's ironic really, considering that he wasn't even around for the first five years. (It feels wrong joking about that, but it was just such an obvious joke.)

I found the right one and it had lots of little envelopes to hold keepsakes and plenty of space to document each milestone they met in incredible detail. I even ended up getting my second born the exact same book, so it wouldn't cause any sibling rivalry along the way. (Why is your book bigger than mine? Why does your book have a ribbon bookmark and mine doesn't? Why does yours have a tap-dancing monkey on the cover and mine has a sleeping sheep?) I'll do almost anything to avoid having to hear questions like that.

Before I had a baby, I thought I'd fill out every detail. I've always loved writing, obviously, and I've always kept journals of my own. I remember with my own baby book, asking my mum why she drew around my hand rather than doing a paint handprint. Now I just think she did well to even do that. There are huge, gaping blanks in my books, and the problem is, I've forgotten half of the details that need to be filled in now. I just hope the parts I have filled in are enough to satisfy my children. I have about three hampers filled with their artwork from over the years. I have plenty of handprints and fingerprints in there and paint splats and every kind of craft we ever did together. (Well, not every single one, because that would fill a whole county.) I think the problem with parenthood is that you'll always feel like you've neglected something. You might have lots of quality time, but you don't have a clean house. You might have lots of day trips, but then you don't feel like you've had enough downtime together at home. You don't have enough hours in the day to do all the things you want to achieve but you've slept well for once.

You can try to fit in everything you want to do, but I've learnt that is a recipe for disaster, or insanity, at least. You need time to do your own things too or you feel like you've sacrificed every part of who you were before having kids. As selfish as it might sound, filling out baby books every night when my kids are asleep isn't my idea of a good time. It's ok as something to dip in and out of, but it's not how I want to spend every free moment. Maybe the problem is that I have too many projects in my mind – too many projects and not enough time to realise them. And I'm not even talking about all the projects related to my children. I want to write, I want to paint, I want to work on my blog, I want to travel, I want to make videos and take photos, I want to go on day trips and work on the garden. I want to read a million books, and I'm not even meeting my monthly target. There just aren't enough hours in a life and kids are very time consuming.

So, the baby books remain patchy. I have tried to scribble in as much information as I can remember, but it isn't done neatly, and it wouldn't win me any parenting award. I used to beat myself up for that kind of stuff, but life's too short to torture yourself over the physical things. Maybe it's a depressing way to look at things, but eventually, the baby books will probably be lost, faded or thrown away, but our memories will be in our minds forever. As I always say to my mum: we're all going to die anyway. I know - what an uplifting thought! At least it removes any guilt with regards to my having a clear-out.

I grew up in a house where meaning was placed on possessions. There were good things about this. For example, we took care of our things and treated them with respect, we knew to be gentle with our belongings and we didn't break anything. But the bad side to that is that you get unhealthily attached to items that you could lose (or stand to lose.) It only takes one thing going wrong to lose all your belongings, but you keep the thoughts in your head. There was a time when I lost nearly everything I owned, and I had to start over. Before that moment, I would have struggled to throw out any of the items I lost, thinking that I needed them. Now, I never think of those "indispensable" objects. I guess they weren't important after all and losing them didn't do anything other than make me feel lighter. I like the idea of condensing my life into a backpack, but I'm still too much of a clutter bug to achieve that. It's still heartening to know that if I had to, I could get by without any of it though, and losing it all again wouldn't devastate me. I hope to pass that on to my kids. I think that's better than making them feel burdened by their belongings. Although, saying that, they must have a genetic predisposition to collecting things, because they both frequently come up with reasons why we can't throw out rubbish. "We could make something out of it," is one of their favourite phrases. I like that frugal mindset too. As long as we aren't found buried under rubbish, I guess they might as well enjoy refashioning boxes into doll's houses and new modes of transportation.

Chapter Twenty-Eight – What Next?

"So, what are we going to do now?" asks my daughter as she exits a six-hour long summer scheme with drum workshops, games, a tuck shop and a water fight. She's already had a change of clothes because of the day's activities, but still, it's never enough. I never remember asking my mum what we were doing next. I probably did and I've just wiped it out of my memory, but I find it so weird the way kids don't count an outing as enough anymore. We used to save day trips for the weekend and the holidays. We just spent every day in the house, in the garden or playing in the street. I think that's a big part of the problem nowadays: a lot of kids can't play in the street because it isn't safe to do so anymore. Maybe it wasn't safe enough in the nineties either, but people just didn't hover like helicopters over the kids as much. But there definitely is far more traffic nowadays and kids don't have the street sense to cope with it. I actually know of a couple of people that have been knocked down, so it does happen. I'm not one of those parents that needs to be in their kids' faces every minute of the day. In fact, I think they need space to create and to think – or more accurately, to fight and to break more springs in my bed with their gymnastic performances. Still, I wouldn't let them play in the street. We live on a busy road that's far too narrow for two-way traffic. It's just too risky and there are no other kids out there, so there isn't even safety in numbers. So, they play in our back garden instead, but obviously this limits their social opportunities to each other, me and one of our neighbours. Maybe that's why they're so dissatisfied with the programme of events I've created. They rely on it entirely to fill every waking moment. If I was sitting around waiting to be taken out instead of being thrown out into the street and told not to come back until dinner time, I'd probably be asking what we were doing too. Nineties parents were lucky in that respect. They were probably the last generation of parents that didn't have to spend much time with their kids. (I'm joking – I think.) But too much togetherness is most definitely a thing. When you can quote someone's every comment before it exits their mouth, you know you've been spending too much time with that person.

I have a much higher tolerance for my kids' company than for adult company, even though spending a lot of time with kids makes me desperate for adult company. Maybe it's because I know the kids are going to bed at half seven. I don't know what I'll do when that comes to an end. When people tell me about how they sit up until half ten watching TV with their kids and hanging out until their own bedtime, I grimace at the thought of it. I'll never understand how some adults manage an entire day without a shred of alone time without cracking up. Maybe it's just dependent on your disposition, or how much you're interacting with your kids when they're awake.

When I was little, my granny always told me that school years were the best days of your life. I found it particularly weird that she said that, considering the fact she was attending school during a world war and was evacuated from Glasgow to Northern Ireland because of it. Sometimes she made flippant remarks, so you couldn't place too much weight on what she said. But she had a way of phrasing everything that turned every one of her comments into a catchphrase. Her accent probably helped with that too. I'd never met another Scottish person in Northern Ireland, so at that time, I suppose it stood out more. No one else wanted to come to Northern Ireland then because the Troubles were still ongoing, and frankly, the place was a hole. I still find it strange, thinking of Belfast as a tourist location, but the number of bus tours and foreign languages present in town confirms that it must be *now*. Anyway, I always hated as a kid when adults said things like that to you. It felt like they didn't appreciate the difficulties of your position, and there are plenty of difficulties that come with being a kid. Not getting to make a single decision for yourself, even when you're at an age when you consider yourself to be capable of it isn't pleasant. I'm sure I have fallen into many adult traps that were laid out generations before I was born. It's weird the way you give birth and the next minute you're talking about how money doesn't grow on trees and how everyone's eye is going to get poked out with a stick turned sword. You rolled your eyes when you heard them as a kid, and then you find yourself saying them, and you don't know what on Earth happened to you. But I know I will never speak wistfully about how easy the school years were. I will never forget them well enough to be fooled into thinking that they were easy. There was too much humiliation to be found there, too much awkwardness and too many pieces of coursework I dreaded doing. Your time isn't your own. Even when you find freedom at the end of the school day; you have to make your journey home (some longer than others, but mine was a trek) and then you have to start into your homework – all for little or no payment.

OK, maybe we got some pocket money, and we had a free bus pass (if you lived far enough away from your school to qualify for one) but there was nothing to buy at the time anyway. Where were you going to go in the late nineties in Belfast when you were underaged and coffee shops weren't a phenomenon yet? Sometimes I miss the freedom and simplicity of that time, but the things we were allowed to do were seriously limited by parental curtailments. Anyway, I know I'm meandering here, but my point is: I understand that being a kid isn't easy, and there are so many new complications now that didn't exist when I was little. I don't want to become out of touch with all the difficult moments involved in growing up. Gladly, I can still remember being that age with clarity and what a confusing time it was. That's what makes it weirder that I'm unconsciously coming out with key phrases my own parents used. Maybe that was how it happened to them too: they were listening to their parents repeating them ad nauseum, and then they found them falling out of their own mouths too. But as a parent, they take on a different meaning that they didn't hold for kids. Now I can see that they really could skewer an eyeball with a jagged stick if they aren't careful, or that they've turned my living room upside down and it does resemble a pigsty, and that I'm the one that will end up clearing it all up. That also eats into my much-needed alone time, so I feel like it's deserving of a phrase that I know counts as nagging.

I know what it's like to have time stretch before you interminably. I feel that way half the time as an adult. As a single parent, it's particularly obvious. When no one is coming home at six to share dinner with and there are no real interruptions to break up the day, it does feel long. I still hate the word "bored" though. Probably because I have felt something I could liken to deep boredom, but that was probably depression, and I've had to fill so many empty moments. Now I can see that boredom really is just underusing your creativity. I want my kids to feel bored because it's a gift that gives you the skills to entertain yourself, and to avoid loneliness too. If you're busy creating, you don't have time to feel desperately lonely because you're directing it all into whatever project you've made for yourself. I guess it would be a lot to try to explain this to kids, so it's easier to just tell them not to use the word "bored." Sometimes it isn't that adults think that kids won't understand; it's that they don't have the energy to put into explaining a concept that it would take all day to describe. When you've been answering questions since before you opened your eyes, the answers to those questions just aren't as interesting to you as the prospect of sitting in silence. But even though I can see the adult side and the child side, it doesn't always help my parenting. I just end up in turmoil, caught

129

somewhere between the two perspectives, trying to be sympathetic to both.

When I was little, there was a little girl my age that I played with a lot. Her parents were always working in her family's business, so they weren't there very much. I guess her granny was technically in the building because she was in an attached granny flat. But I distinctly remember seeing the lady at my friend's birthday party and it was like a celebrity sighting because I'd only seen her that one time after years of visiting there, so clearly there was no parental supervision there. I can still remember watching Thomas the Tank Engine and Alice in Wonderland while my five-year-old friend cooked a roast dinner for her parents coming home. I know we don't give kids enough credit nowadays for what they are capable of, but I'm still not letting mine play out in the street. At least not until my daughter stops trying to throw herself into oncoming traffic each time she sees a "bestie" on the other side of the road. Sometimes the silliness outweighs the trust, and that's not my fault as a parent, I think.

So, I guess I'll either have to try to keep coming up with the goods regarding family outings and craft projects – that or let my kids wallow in their own boredom and sink to fighting each other for entertainment. I suppose somewhere in the middle would be the healthiest answer.

I still meet some children that have that kind of idyllic nineties childhood where they call on their friends and play on the road, rarely having to stand in for a passing car. But I don't want to live in Saintfield – that's the bottom line. I grew up in the place and I spent eighteen years waiting to get out of it. That's the kind of place you have to move to if you want to find that way of life. That, or you need to have money. I don't have that either, so I guess this city-living containment to the back yard and walks to the park lifestyle is the one for us. I suspect my kids' expectations are so high by this point that even if a child's entertainer arrived daily, equipped with a bouncy castle, the ability to make every balloon animal under the sun and an unrivalled talent for face painting that surpassed any other living painter, they would still get bored with them. As they put the first brushstroke to my kids' faces, they'd probably turn to me and say "Mummy, what are we doing after this?"

I'd take it a step further than that. God forbid there was ever an emergency, but if there was and I was hospitalised, they'd probably ask me the minute I was discharged, "Mummy, what are we doing after this?

Keelan LaForge

Chapter Twenty-Nine – Introductions to Sleepovers

Why is it that your idea of fun changes so drastically as an adult? I used to be amazed by a friend I had in school's parents. They were happy to have about twelve additional kids over a night and they bought takeaway pizzas for the whole crew, never worrying what the cost would be. They weren't well off either, but they were generous and didn't seem to place any value on money. They were hippies really. Maybe they were secretly getting stoned when we were all messing around in their daughters' bedroom, doing each other's make-up, and not going to sleep until 3AM. As a teenager, I thought it was wonderful. We had a type of freedom I didn't have at home. My dad was always a tidy person, and he didn't want his living quarters or his sleep routine to be disturbed by our social lives. My mum was more laid back, but she was always trying not to annoy him, mainly because he had such a demanding job. So, we kept the noise down, and I can recall having a sleepover on one occasion – but it never happened again. We slept in the living room so we wouldn't keep my dad up and I remember having a pronounced feeling of stress about the noise levels for most of it. So, it was like a holiday staying at my friend's house. Her parents just didn't care. They would have let us do anything. They weren't there half the time, so we just helped ourselves to takeaway or improvised with whatever food happened to be in the cupboards. Kids really don't care how fancy a place is; they just want to have fun there. Even though they had quite hippy-like values, they had strong morals too, so things didn't get too out of control. I do remember one occasion on which we tried to go to a club, failed and ended up under a bridge. I'm guessing most kids have drunk alcohol under a bridge at one point in their years of rebellion, but the funny thing was, I didn't even have a drink while I was there. I was too much of a goodie two shoes at that point. I still ended up stranded in a coffee shop when I decided to absent myself from the rest of the night's activities and my mum probably had to pick me up. I didn't live close to the city, so if you didn't want to go along with what your friends were doing and it was after a certain hour, you were a bit screwed.

Thankfully, I'm not at that stage with my kids yet. I hope that when I get there, I'll either be a willing taxi provider or that I'll be ok with them embracing their freedom. But we have started small with their first sleepovers. This week, they've had their cousin to stay, and they've had a ball. She's only a few years younger than them and they play together so well. They think it's great fun and they anticipate the next sleepover before the current one has even ended. I enjoy them too, but bedtime is a bit of a nightmare. I agreed that the bottom bunk would be shared between the two younger ones. I thought it would help to train my daughter to finally stay in her own bed, and the first night, it worked like a charm. It took them about two and half hours to go to sleep, but when they did, they were like two sleeping angels all night. It was a special kind of bliss I haven't experienced in nearly a decade. Broken sleep has just become an accepted part of my life – not appreciated – but accepted.

I don't know if I'll ever find the sleepover phase fun when the kids are teenagers. It feels like sleepovers have become something much more dangerous lately. In recent years, with the public exposure of so much depravity in human nature, I don't think I could trust many people to mind my kids overnight. I'm glad those arguments haven't started yet.

Anyway, last night, at their mini sleepover, the kids were so excited. I was surprised they weren't more tired than they were, especially after such a busy day of play and a summer scheme to wear them out. Two of them even asked to go for a nap as it was approaching bedtime, so I had to hold them off. I was hopeful they'd go over as soon as their heads hit the pillows, but no. You should never assume anything about kids. Every time you think you've sorted something out in advance, it never works out as planned. It had been a full-on day, but I'd been daydreaming about bedtime and the activities I had planned for myself once the kids were sleeping. But alas, it was not to be. (I never thought I'd use that word in a sentence, but there's a first time for everything.) It was hard to quell the giggling. Once one started, it was like a ripple effect. They wouldn't lie down in bed, and they always do when there are just two of them for their "getting to sleep" story.

"I'm getting out of bed to see the pictures," my niece announced.

The girls both laughed because this idea was foreign to them. Once they lie down and the lights go out, I read them a pictureless book on my Kindle, or from their collection of novels they don't have the patience to read by themselves.

"There aren't any pictures!" said my daughter.

My niece whispered in her ear, but it was audible from where I was.

"We can wait until Auntie Keelan leaves and then I'll look at the pictures."

That produced another round of hysterics. I would have found it hilarious too if I wasn't in my bedtime mood. My bedtime mood is a level I've reached where I no longer have a sense of humour and I have a strong need to get everyone to go to sleep and shush so I can embark on my plans for the evening. I was ready to do a work-out, have a shower and I was contemplating adding another layer of paint to a picture I'd been working on. I had so much to do, I wondered how I'd fit it all in before eleven PM. I was just hoping the story would put them to sleep. I was wondering if Winnie the Witch was filled with too much excitement for them. I needed a slower story with less action, so I read from a magazine of short stories that the girls didn't have a great deal of interest in. That started the pictures problem again, because it became evident to my niece that it contained coloured pictures. But I just kept advising her to lie down and I hid the pictures. She and my younger daughter had decided to share a pillow after finding top to toe too annoying the previous evening. That way, no one kicked each other in the face and there seemed to be fewer complaints. They both sat up tens of times to have a drink of water. I could hardly blame them. It was the hottest week of the year. A huge heatwave had come, and I'd had to open all the windows just so we could breathe. But they had requested I close the bedroom window again because we have some loutish neighbours out the back that get drunk and shout at their friends, and at each other all night every time there's the slightest hint of sunshine. I managed to block out some of the noise, but there are probably people angrily shutting windows streets away because of the same couple.

"We can't get to sleeeeeep," the girls whined. "The people are too noisy. They're keeping us awake."

I knew that was bull. They hadn't even attempted to close their eyes once. They'd barely been horizontal since we'd been in the room. Reading in a calm and bored tone wasn't working its usual magic. They just wouldn't stop talking and giggling. I got to my feet and announced that stories were over and started to threaten keeping them home from the summer club they were due to attend the following morning. It was half past eight and the whole thing was eating into my valuable yoga time. That always puts me in a bad mood. I think it's the fact that you've made so much self-sacrifice all day for the children's sake, and they don't even see it. Then, when you finally think you're going to have a moment alone to gather your thoughts, they intrude on that too. They just think we're all having a great time and they don't seem to notice that I'm not. I find it weird, considering the fact that my "I've had enough face" probably looks similar to my "just given birth" face. Parenting is the mental version of giving birth, but without the end in sight part, I suppose.

I let everyone go to the bathroom again, which took about twenty-five minutes. I should have made them go one at a time, but I didn't think of that until they were underway with the whole thing. I tucked the girls in for the "final" time, warning them that if they didn't go to sleep, they wouldn't be going to the club or having another sleepover that week. We had one planned for two days later.

I went downstairs and told myself if I just imagined them all sleeping soundly, it would happen. I tried to focus on my work-out video and feeling the burn, but I couldn't even concentrate on the discomfort. I could hear footsteps upstairs – not like someone quietly padding about. It sounded like there was an army of them on the loose. I wondered how on Earth parents had ever controlled the behaviour of such children. I never saw defiance like it when I was a kid – or if you did, it was so rare that you wrote that kid off as a bad egg.

I closed the living room door, hoping if they reappeared that they'd take the hint. Then, I started my yoga routine. It was intensive and it felt good to get rid of some of the frustration held inside my body. But before I had managed to finish it – and it was only a fifteen-minute work-out, I heard knocking on the door.

"We can't sleep," called my daughter. She seemed to have gained extra confidence from having her cousin around. It's weird the way they come downstairs together, like wolves in packs, ready for attack. I wasn't ready for it. I paused the video and slumped as I walked to the door.

"Why are you up?" I asked, only opening the door a fraction of a centimetre. I don't know what the point in that was; it wasn't like they were just going to give up and go away. When I was a kid, a closed door meant "don't even think about coming in," but to them it means "a closed door that can easily be opened" – ie: we might as well remove all the doors and have an open plan everything.

135

They waited expectantly in my path. "Auntie Keelan," said my niece. "The girls are keeping me up."

I knew that wasn't the full story, but it was a good two thirds of it. I escorted them back to bed and they made the obligatory trip to the toilet. It's a good job we don't get charged for water here – that's all I have to say. I waited until they were finished and then tucked them into bed again, giving them another ineffectual warning.

I went downstairs. I'd been delaying my post work-out shower because I'd worried that it would wake them up when they'd just got settled, but that was no longer a concern. I decided to just go ahead with it. When I went upstairs, they were in the bathroom again anyway. I let them go one more time, wondering how a human bladder could possibly produce that much liquid, but I knew it was better to be on the safe side. Then I kicked them out of the bathroom and told them they'd better be asleep by the time I got out of the shower. I could hear giggling through the bathroom door, but I just tried to pretend I didn't hear it. I got lost for a few seconds in the lavender scented steam that filled the shower. If I closed my ears, I could almost pretend I was in a spa for a minute. But the bulging vein in my forehead said otherwise. I was so tired, in body and soul. When bedtime isn't adhered to, I get more than ratty. It's just one of those things I can't lighten up about. Even on holiday, I can't cope with the routine being messed with. Maybe I'm just incredibly selfish about my alone time. But there's nothing more beautiful in life than the feeling you get after putting your kids to bed. You know everyone is safe and you can truly relax. When it doesn't go to plan, the stress hits you like a breeze block falling from the sky.

When I came out of the bathroom, I hoped to see them all sleeping soundly, but it wasn't to be.

"Mummy, can you read to us again?"

"No," I said, feeling mean. I never like to turn my kids down when they ask for a story. But I was tired of reading. It hadn't been relaxing, shouting the story out, syllable by syllable, just to be heard above all the chit chat. I doubted anyone had heard what happened to the protagonist in the end anyway.

I barked at them to stay in bed and announced that the bathroom was closed, except for real emergencies.

"What's an emergency?" my daughter asked.

Sometimes I swear they ask questions like that just to stall me. They know the answers are long-winded and require thought and time. That's the only reason they ask them. I don't believe in curiosity after eight PM; they're just playing you so they can get another minute or hour of time awake.

I walked downstairs, exasperated and calling "good night" for the fiftieth time. Then, I had to ask myself, was it really a good night? In two hours, I had achieved a quarter of what I planned to do. I'd probably got my step count up for the day though, with all the trips up and down the stairs. I poured myself a glass of Bailey's and added ice. It happened to be the year's heatwave that week too, so the sweat was rolling off you minutes after having a shower. That probably didn't help the situation, I thought. If I struggled to sleep through it as an adult, how did I expect kids to do it? They had kicked all the covers off, but they were still probably burning up. We didn't have air conditioning since sunshine and heat is a once-a-year phenomenon in Belfast. I could see the kids' point of view, but I just wasn't in a patient mood. I've always thought I was alone in that because it's something no parents talk openly about. Maybe they worry it might sound a bit like they don't want to spend time with their kids if they say it out loud. The problem is most of us probably do spend a lot of time with our kids – too much according to a study I recently read. I came across it in a magazine one day. It said that parents spend several more hours a day with their children, compared with fifty years ago. Even though there were far more housewives then and far fewer employed women, they still didn't see their children half as much as we do. We are unique in the level of care we give our children these days. Often, they used to just fend for themselves. Now, everyone's child is sewn to their butt. So, I finally arrive at the conclusion that it's ok that I want them to stay in bed, and that it isn't a reflection on how much time I want to spend with them. The evenings are meant to be adult time.

They still weren't asleep. I could hear them padding around upstairs, but I tried to ignore it. I turned on a documentary on Netflix – the one about the guy that killed his dad. I tried to channel my frustration into that and the psychological breakdown of the whole event. Maybe that's why I write psychological fiction actually – it gives me somewhere to direct all the anger and frustration that has nowhere else to turn at 10PM when I still haven't had a chance to drink my tea without being summoned upstairs.

I went upstairs a couple more times to tell everyone to get out of the bathroom. I felt like padlocking it and adding an "out of order" sign. They were out of order in my view; they were still worryingly giddy for ten PM. I hoped they'd crash soon from sheer exhaustion. I was thinking about going to bed too, but I didn't like going up when they were still awake. It just resulted in everyone moving into my bed, or the demands doubling because they knew I was right next door, and I could respond quicker.

Finally, they all fell asleep nearing half ten. I knew they'd all be shattered the next day, but there was nothing I could have done to get them to sleep any sooner – besides buying a tranquiliser gun anyway.

I dread to think what they'd be like if I allowed them to have a friend to stay each. I wish I could be one of those Nintendo Switch reliant parents that couldn't care less when their kids go to bed, but I can't relax until they're asleep. It's a curse, but I guess, in a way, I'd rather be that way.

Chapter Thirty – The Wildness

"She's wild," says my dad. That's what he says when he thinks someone's behaviour is laughably unbelievable. He says it at least once a week about my younger daughter. We usually see him once a week. She always does say the first thing that comes out of her mouth. Sometimes, I doubt whether she actually places any meaning on what she says. I think she just says something on the spur of the moment and forgets it as soon as it leaves her mouth.

I remember walking her to P1 after half term. She had been off school for a week, and we had gone on a local holiday together. The week had been filled with child-friendly activities, and it was probably any kid's idea of bliss.

"Will you be happy to get a break from me?" I asked her, joking.

"What do you think?" she said, looking me dead in the eyes, her eyebrows raised.

I burst out laughing, but there was something unnerving about it too. I think she has inherited that paternal tendency to look straight through you as she delivers a perfectly sarcastic comment. She's always been like that – well – since she learned how to speak anyway. I always find that her cheek increases with the backing of others. Maybe that's true of all kids, but she really loves an audience.

I envy her bouncy vitality sometimes, and the fact that she's so quick with a remark. I haven't achieved that to anywhere near the same degree after three and a half decades on Earth. I guess those things are inbuilt – like an eye colour or an affinity for science. I wish I had a tenth of the confidence she does.

She was talking to her older sister about a girl in her class. She had told my younger daughter that the girl had recently disclosed that she didn't like her. It didn't seem to have much of an impact at the time, but she'd obviously considered it since.

"It's not very nice that "insert name" doesn't like me," she said, over dinner. They were meant to be eating and I'd used the phrase "less talking, more eating" about fifty-seven times – no exaggeration. But they continued their conversation like I wasn't there. I often wonder at what age the ability to eat and talk at the same time kicks in. It must be something that takes a while to master because I never see my kids doing it. Strangely, they are able to talk and mess around at the table though. They're good at that sort of multitasking. They also never seem to have any bother eating sweets and watching TV at the same time. They often fight while they're doing it too. They must have a particular talent for that kind of multitasking.

The conversation continued. I'd heard my older daughter say that particular girl didn't like her sister before. I wasn't exactly sure why, or how they'd established an unfavourable rapport in the few moments spent in each other's company before the drop off in the morning. Maybe she thought she was just an annoying younger sibling.

"It's not that she doesn't like you," my daughter said, somewhat diplomatically. "It's just that she thinks you're a bit … small."

"She should like me," continued my younger daughter. "I'm the cutest kid in the world." I was starting to realise which quality it might have been that led to a certain feeling of dislike from the girl.

"What about me?" asked my older daughter.

"You're the second cutest," my daughter said, without a moment's hesitation.

That seemed to satisfy her sister, who frequently gushes about how cute her younger sibling is, hugging her tightly and talking about her like she's five years her junior, rather than sixteen months. They're almost the same height and my younger daughter can hold her own – apart from where squabbles over the remote control are concerned. My older daughter has established her supremacy where that is concerned.

Their tabletop chatter always makes me laugh, even though their table manners often make me want to cry. The ones that rile me the most are feet on the wall, feet on the table, throwing food, eating dishes like a roast dinner with their hands, constant "high jinks," like my granny would have said, that entirely interfere with their eating. Another dislike of mine is when they move pieces of food they don't like off their plate and onto the table so I have something else to clean – as if there wasn't enough already. The whole process is mostly maddening. Sometimes there are the rare redeeming moments when they eat more than usual. It was particularly satisfying this week when they ate my meatloaf because I didn't expect them to touch it – other than to prod it with an investigative finger, at least. Those moments really stay in your mind because they are so rare and unexpected. Usually, if they have any compliments for the chef, it's because we're eating takeaway.

My kids still say their favourite meal in the world is McDonald's. My older daughter has just realised that if she sacrifices the Happy Meal toy for an "adult's meal" she gets the opportunity to have Coke rather than a "baby drink." Little does she know I'm ordering her meal off the savers' menu, so it actually costs less than a Happy Meal does. It works out better for both of us. I'm partial to a McDonald's too. I always have been. Truth be told, I don't really care how unhealthy it is – it tastes great to me. I'd rather not analyse the nutritional contents in case it puts me off – which it probably wouldn't anyway. I'm bad at compartmentalising my problems, but I'm good at compartmentalising what I don't want to know when it comes to food. I guess greed wins every time. I tried and failed at vegetarianism as a teenager and I haven't looked back since.

There is something nostalgic about McDonald's. I equally associate it with my childhood and my kids' childhood. There aren't many things like that that still endure. I used to go with my mum, and I remember the joy of getting a Happy Meal toy. Although then, they were made of durable non-environmentally friendly plastic, but no one knew or cared about that then. I have fond memories of the drive thru on the road between our house and Belfast. I remember one time my mum drove into it when, unbeknownst to us, it was closed, and she had to reverse back out again. That drive through went in an entire circle, so it was funny watching her navigating that, and the accompanying language would have been fully muted with beeps before the watershed. Another time, we all got one of the 99p cheeseburgers as a "quick snack." None of us felt satisfied after it, so we went back round again. "Déjà vu," said the man at the order window. They practically knew us on a first name basis.

I don't know if my kids and I are quite at that point of desperation for a McDonald's, but we do frequent it each month. It's probably a sin that I don't yet have the rewards app, come to think of it. We were devastated when they increased the cheeseburger price to £1.29. It felt like the end of an era. We should probably get a grip, considering the fact it's still about nine pounds cheaper than a burger anywhere else. I love the way the girls' faces light up when I take them there. They get that look of excitement you usually only see in their eyes when you do something big – like going on holiday or entering a water park. The novelty never wears off. I like a Big Mac too. When I lived in Paris, I was right next door to McDonald's. At the time, my friend stayed with me every weekend and we got the two-burger deal they had then when we were hungover. It was a great cure for nausea, surprisingly enough. It's one of those institutions that feels like it's always been there and serves as a bit of reassurance on a bad day when everything is unravelling around you, that some things never change.

Chapter Thirty-One – Saying a Little Prayer

I always pray with my kids before they go to sleep. I was raised as a strict Christian, but I haven't imposed any of those beliefs on them. Mostly because I shrugged them all off at the age of sixteen when I was in my rebellious phase. (Has that ever ended?) But it's one of those little things I can't quite let go of. I hope it's a comfort to them, whether they believe in the rest of it or not. Mostly, it's just a chance to connect with them and ask for things that make them more likely to go to bed. (Please give the girls good dreams and keep them in their own beds all night – that last bit is just for me and probably proves that there isn't a higher power because they never do that.)

Unfortunately, my vision of the night-time routine isn't quite like theirs. I imagine that I tuck them into bed, they listen intently while I pray and read a quick story and then they fall into a peaceful sleep within minutes. Usually, the whole thing takes about an hour, and they try every possible ruse to drag it out even longer. Recently, they've realised that if they say a prayer of their own, it buys them a few extra minutes, so they've started doing that too. I don't want to hurry them through it in case I somehow crush their spirits, so I indulge them, but they just become more and more ridiculous and meandering – like a drink fuelled anecdote with no end to it.

"Dear God, please look after all of us and let us have a nice sleep. Look after our family (and they proceed to list every member of the extended family, including said relatives' feline friends.) Help me not to poop my pants," they say, or something else related to toilet activities. Shrieks of laughter ensue, which lead to another ten-minute wind down where I tell them to "settle down" and "shush." I always descend the stairs with a strong need for wine and the kind of quiet where you can hear nothing but your own breath.

Sometimes you do things for your kids without even stopping to question it. It's just something you did as a kid yourself. I try to pass on what I think were the positive aspects of my childhood, without the accompanying negative parts. Maybe all parents are constantly striving to do that. I often wonder how many of them manage to pull it off. Are we always giving our kids some sort of inner conflict that they'll have to address in therapy a decade or two from now, even when we're actively trying to avoid such a thing? These are the parenting questions I always ask myself in empty moments (of which, in that respect, thankfully, there are very few.) Hopefully they don't grow up to be like the people in a Netflix documentary I recently watched "Keep Sweet, Pray and Obey." (It's about a so-called Christian cult that brainwashed its members.) I hope that they feel like the beliefs they choose to take on haven't been forced on them. But I'm sure I'll have done something wrong. I think it's impossible not to. I'm sure I'll be reprimanded for it a few years from now – probably publicly and dramatically, knowing the girls.

In the meantime, their prayers give me a laugh at times. The other night, my daughter prayed for everyone in the world, and then said, "I love everyone in the world – apart from the people I don't know and the bad guys in jail." Then she interrupted herself to ask me, "Do you know anyone in jail?" I had a quiet moment where I hoped that an affirmative answer to that couldn't be applied to her dad.

Chapter Thirty-Two – Making a *** of Yourself

Sometimes as a parent, you have to take a stand. Maybe something crops up that you consider to be unjust or thoughtless and you suddenly feel you have a responsibility to address such issues. You want things to be corrected in society for your offspring and their friends. You're not just speaking up for yourself anymore – it's a societal and intergenerational thing. When my daughter first started in P1, I was shocked to learn about the teachers' presents system. At Christmas time and at the end of the year, the parents band together to create a gift fund for the teachers and classroom assistants. I'd never heard of that before. When I was in school, the teachers were lucky if their efforts were rewarded with an apple and a dog-eared, handmade card. At first, when I heard about the gift fund, I thought it was a practical and money-saving idea. If we all grouped together to contribute to a present, the £5 we might have spent would become £1 and the present we were able to get would be much better. But I didn't know how it worked yet. So, when they suggested we contribute ten pounds each, I was shocked. It seemed unfathomable to me that a teacher might get a bonus of several hundred pounds on top of their salary. I know they work hard for that money but coming from the assumption that they just got a coffee mug and an apple, it seemed crazed to me. I told my friend about it. She had more experience because her son was two years ahead of my oldest daughter in school.

"Oh, yeah, I know – it's a lot. Someone asked for a contribution of twenty per parent last year."

"Have you ever said anything about it?"

"I just pay it now and don't question it. It just seems to be what they do at that school."

I wasn't in the mood to remain silent then. I wanted to speak up for all the parents that might be struggling to get by. Having your kids in school was expensive enough for something that was supposed to be free. Between spending a hundred quid on a uniform, fifty on school shoes, the school fund and then all the other items that needed to be sent in, it was barely manageable. Some families live on a shoestring budget, but evidently none of them were in the surrounding area of that school district – or if they were, they had been smoothed over and forgotten about – like unwanted ripples in salon-straightened hair. (Probably belonging to the exact parents in that social bracket.)

I asked my mum what she made of it all. She had a loud opinion, looking from the inside, out. She was a teacher herself - albeit a secondary one. She said she was lucky if she got a "thank you" from her pupils and then she went off on a rant for a long time about modern day manners and the collapse of civilised society. I still went with her reaction because it matched up with my own instinctive reaction. It was decided – I was going to say something, not just for myself, but for the benefit of all financially struggling parents in our community.

I opened the group chat. "Ten pounds is quite a lot to ask of people, especially near Christmas time. For some families, that's the difference between eating and not eating dinner that day."

I hoped that the truth in what I was saying would sink in with someone. Maybe everyone would come to their senses and lower it to a five-pound contribution, which would still result in £150 for the teacher and classroom assistant. I still thought that was generous.

It didn't exactly go to plan. Sometimes when you make a mission out of something, it comes back to bite you in the bum.

There was a deathly quiet – like an awkward silence that could be felt even through the medium of WhatsApp. Then, I got a response – although silence might have been preferrable.

"Well, good luck to you finding something for less than ten pounds by yourself."

I could read the anger in her message. I didn't know the lady's name, so I couldn't place where the comment had come from. I thought it best that she hopefully didn't know mine either. It would have been awkward if we ended up exchanging pleasantries on the school run. Maybe, I thought, in that case, I could tell her I have an alter-ego that only comes out online. I could just blame it on that – like an evil twin whose actions I could abdicate all responsibility for. That's the problem. I have this deep-rooted need to address injustice in life, or what I perceive to be unjust – however small it might be. But I also have a need to people please in person. It's easy to stand up for issues at a remove, but when you have to say hello to the same person you just confronted by text, it's a different story. It didn't get me anywhere anyway. I ended up in B&M looking for acceptable teacher and classroom assistant gifts that got the balance right between not looking cheap and not coming to a total of more than ten pounds. I had to prove that lady wrong in my own mind. It was petty of me, but it felt like I'd committed myself to taking a stand.

Since that, I hope I've grown up a bit. I've learnt that you just have to suck up the costs sometimes, regarding your children. Sometimes, they just want to be the same as everyone else, so you have to park your battles, for their sake. I also don't want to be that mouthy mother that embarrasses them everywhere they go. So, I shut up and pay the piper – most of the time. Now and again, I'll decide I want to search for a more personal present, and those have been well received too. Ultimately, it doesn't matter what you get the teacher as a present – so long as you give it kindly and without making it into the cause of outrage – whether your own or other parents'.

It turns out that sometimes it's better to sit there and shut up than to take a stand. I'll reserve my stand-taking for the issues that really matter and on which I can actually make a difference, like my refusal to visit the ice-cream shop outside my kid's school on a daily basis.

Chapter Thirty-Three – Real Mess over Fake Tidiness

I hate our garden. I know I should love it, and there are many moments when the sun warms my face as I sit with a cup of coffee at our decomposing garden table and I can almost imagine I'm somewhere pleasant, but it's a hard place to like. One of the specifications I had the last time we moved house was "must have a garden." I didn't mind how small it was; I just needed an outdoor space to send my kids to when they had more energy than sense. And it has served that purpose, so for that, I am grateful. The main problem with it is that it is on a slant, and the concrete must have been laid in the garden the year that concrete was invented, because it has worn away to almost nothing and always ends up with a dirty coating – the origins of which are still a mystery to me five years later. Every time it rains, the garden becomes a complete swamp. Each time the girls come inside, even after five minutes of play out there, they look like they've been mud wrestling. I sweep it and do what I can with it. Sometimes, there are even sunny spells in Northern Ireland when the ground starts to dry out and we almost get a glimpse of what the concrete could have once looked like. But that layer of dirt is always there. The sludge makes it a playground for snails. There are more snails out there than public health hazards, and that's really saying something. I've found several frogs frolicking out there too and I'm sure there are many other species of pond life having a great time. At least someone can safely play in the garden, I guess – until the neighbour's cat gets them, at least.

Over the years, I have tried to cull the weeds, but what is a huge undertaking only ends in complete regrowth a week later. I tried to beautify the garden with some flowers a few years ago, but I have since given up because the weeds are quick to strangle whatever life might try to emerge there. I do have a hardy lavender plant that has somehow survived, a foxglove that moves its location in the garden without human intervention each summer and fuchsia that has been there far longer than me. It's a 1920's house, so the plants could have been there longer than my grandparents were on the face of the Earth, for all I know. When I arrived, there was a dead sycamore tree in the corner of the garden. It looked like it had been choked to death by ivy and I don't know what it was about it, but it attracted hundreds of bees. Maybe there was a hive buried in there under the matted ivy. You could have hidden a dead body in there, after all, and no one ever would have known.

After years of having all sunlight blocked by the corpse of that tree, my landlord agreed to cut it down. It mainly became pressing because of the influx of bees, and that, combined with my kids playing outside presented certain dangers. The neighbours behind me were overjoyed when it was chopped down. They had complained about the tree before to me, and about the fact that it blocked the sunlight out of their garden too. We've spoken a few times, but mostly we just see each other through our kitchen windows every day, which back onto each other. It's like watching people on TV; you forget they're even real humans. When we bump into each other in the street, it's always a bit surreal. Anyway, the day that the tree was removed, I saw them standing at their kitchen window admiring the view and they both gave me the thumbs up and a wave. They must have been waiting for that moment for about forty years. Despite my landlord's claim that there was no hive in the tree, I haven't seen a single bee since its removal. And I'm not against having bumblebees around; it's those hovering ones I can't stand that sit right above your ear when you're trying to read a book and buzz incessantly. My kids were glad the "bees" were gone too. They hadn't been able to use the garden without one bothering them either. I know they say all insects have a purpose and without them, the world wouldn't run as smoothly, but I genuinely believe that insects like that live to annoy people. Now I don't have to deal with my kids running inside every two seconds when they've asked to play in the garden, shouting that they can't go outside again because a bee is going to sting them. I don't even know if those ones had stingers – but they were annoying enough that they probably did have all the equipment.

At least that's one aspect of our garden that I hate that's been eradicated. If I owned it, I'd scrap the whole thing and start over. But I know we're lucky to have an outdoor space at all. It's no more of a health hazard than the house we currently rent is anyway. The girls have spent hours just riding their bikes in a circle there, tossing a ball back and forth until it ends in it going over the neighbour's fence. Now and again, they'll ask why we don't have a swing set or a trampoline like everyone else we know. That has just become the standard garden apparatus these days, but overall, they're happy to poke in the dirt and draw on the ground with chalk. The simplest things really are the ones that stick with them – even if my kids might appear materialistic on the surface.

I think Lockdown helped with that. It reassured me in a way, knowing that we could survive without the little luxuries we have come to rely upon. I was relieved to learn that I could survive without coffee shops. I just recreated them at home. The girls didn't need all the outings we had before. They still speak fondly of that summer spent under duvet covers made into tents and eating picnic lunches at the coffee table they'd pulled into the hall. We did work-out videos together and laughed heartily. We put on a record and did silly dances to old songs. It's true that the free things are the things kids remember. Even when they bring up something we did that did cost money, it's usually a simple moment in that more costly event that stood out to them.

Sometimes you need your kids' reassurance as much as they need yours. Mine often say things to me that save me from one of those pits of desperation I'm almost always falling into. They have rescued me from so many harsh self-judgements – showing me that they don't share the negative view I have of myself. Adults have been conditioned to believe things by the society they've grown up in, and kids haven't got there yet. They are clear-sighted about things that get obscured by the conditioning that has carried us to adulthood.

Since having kids, I have always felt judged for the fact that I "don't work." I dread that question coming up because I know I'll have to supply some sort of justification for it, and nothing is ever adequate to explain why I'm not in office wear or why I don't make use of the overpriced local childcare provider. I always assume that my kids think as little of me as many adults seem to do. I expect them to question why I'm not going out to the typical nine to five, or why I haven't acquired any of the hallmarks of true adulthood, like a mortgage or a paid-off car or a pension plan. My daughter turned to me last week, as she mused about the return to school, and the free time I would find myself with. I expected her to judge me too - or question me about what I'd be doing with my time – what valuable things I'd be achieving in that precious five-hour period. But she didn't.

"Maybe you could go to the spa while we're in school some time. You should do that and relax," she said.

She wanted me to take care of myself and to treat myself in my free time and that comment meant so much to me. It just showed that she didn't condemn me for being a stay-at-home mother, or for spending my free time writing and painting pictures. She thought what I was doing was valuable, that I was working hard and that I deserved a break. Sometimes your kids remind you to be kind to yourself when you otherwise would have been brutal and broken your own spirit.

The same applies to what they expect of your living quarters. Sometimes, my older daughter will complain about the fact that she doesn't have her own room or that we don't have a swimming pool installed in the back yard. But overall, they love the little things. They don't focus on the flaws in the same way adults do. They see opportunity where we see imperfection. They don't focus on the swamp-like surroundings in their garden – they see the mud as material for mud pies and pretend play. I need to tune in to their frequency at times – to remind myself of what's truly important. They always see that much more clearly than I do. It isn't the aesthetics that matter – it's the love shared between family members and the support we give each other. It's the small comment made that uplifts someone that matters – not the quality of your décor or the contents of your purse.

When I've had enough, they remind me to make do with the garden we have and not to allow its flaws to steal any joy from me. They've shown me in their silly, loving - and sometimes annoying behaviour - what I've most needed to learn about myself.

Chapter Thirty-Four – Making a Scene

Sometimes I think kids come along as a reminder to you to stop taking yourself so seriously. If you look around you, you notice just how many adults aren't living fun lives. They keep their heads down, wear their restrictive office wear, they obsess about mortgages and credit card bills and career advancement. But what if we were closer to achieving what we were meant to achieve in life as five-year-olds? We are busy moving forwards, losing ourselves in exams and deadlines and money worries when a little person springs into our life and makes us stop in the street to poke in the dirt and fill our pockets with leaves. Those things are important, even though they might seem trivial to us. We are never too old to cry, or to feel vulnerable, or to laugh at ourselves. An example that illustrates this for me was one day when I was doing the school run. I'd parked the car and I had just crossed the road with the kids and was approaching the school gates – the busiest stretch of the street when my skirt fell around my ankles. It turned out the zip had given in at a bad moment and I dropped to the ground, pulling the girls around me like a human shield while I sorted myself out. I don't know how many people actually noticed it because it was all so quick and shocking, but I always think now that in someone on the school run's mind, I'm probably the woman that lost her skirt in front of everyone. I laughed hysterically the second it happened, which was probably a bad idea because it highlighted the whole thing to anyone that hadn't already noticed, but you have to laugh at how ridiculous you are at times. When I do that and get a laugh from my kids too, it feels like it was worth whatever embarrassment it might have brought me. You're never too old to be embarrassed, to be humbled or to laugh at yourself – and nothing is serious in the future when everyone has forgotten about it.

My older daughter has a sensitive disposition. She was upset this week because she was told off for something that was perpetrated by someone else in school. My younger daughter is definitely much more brazen. I think she was just born with an innate ability to laugh everything off and to stride out into the world, not worrying about taking up too much space.

She decided to choose that moment to own up to the fact that she had been told off that week. It had happened days earlier and it didn't seem to have even registered with her, unlike my other daughter, who seemed deeply affected by her scolding.

"When the teacher isn't looking," my younger daughter said, conspiratorially, "My friend and I do this." She held her arm out in theatrical way, miming like she was singing opera and we all burst out laughing. She's great at turning too much severity into a bit of fun. Since she was already in confession mode, she said, "I never told you, but I got told off in P1 for screaming in the bathroom."

"Why were you screaming in the bathroom?"

"I was screaming my friends' names," she said, laughing, "Like this." She proceeded to shriek loud enough she could probably be heard streets away.

"What did they teacher do?"

"She told me not to let it happen again."

That instruction made me laugh because it sounded like something a team leader in a bank would say to their subordinate – not to a five-year-old. She almost takes a certain pride in admitting to having been chastised; she'll do anything to get a laugh from someone. I just hope healthy limits to that set in before adulthood. But it's something I really admire – her ability to let things wash over her without getting discouraged by things. I can picture her being a comedian when she grows up – one of the ones that turns their so-called failings into really funny jokes. I just hope the next parent-teacher meeting goes ok. I always get the feeling I've dodged a bullet when her school report comes back to me, and it is purely positive. I secretly think she has her priorities right though – laughter, friends and fun are her top three priorities, and it makes me realise how much I deprived myself of those things – just by worrying too much about things I couldn't change anyway. Sometimes you have to do the opera face and make the people around you laugh, even if you get caught and told off for not following every rule to the letter.

Mortified: A Motherhood Memoir

Chapter Thirty-Five – Takeaway for Breakfast, Lunch and Dinner

As a modern-day parent, sometimes it's easy to get lost in the societal standards set up all around you. I forget that I can and should say no to my kids. I often fall victim to the mistake of agreeing to whatever they suggest. It's hard not to get swept up in their confident statements of what we're doing. When I was a kid, I was scared to make any suggestions. I just went along with whatever was mapped out by our parents and met any pleasant surprises along the way with nothing short of glee. For example, if we got a Chinese takeaway, I felt like I'd won the lottery. I relished every bite, and I even treated the drive to and collection from the restaurant with gratitude. I've always loved Chinese food. But I never would have suggested getting it. I just knew not to. That kind of question wasn't in my vernacular. I guess we were well-trained – or no one had as much money then, so no one expected as much.

Now, my kids will, not just suggest, but decide what we're doing – often with the aid of my bank card. I have to stop myself sometimes and think, "wait a minute – I'm the adult here. I can say no."

We rarely get takeaway now – with the cost-of-living crisis and inflation and everything. Mostly, I just refuse to pay upwards of thirty pounds for a substandard burger and chips. It might save you the bother of making it yourself, but since I was gifted my mum's unused deep fat fryer, everything tastes as good at home anyway.

Anyway, on Saturday, I decided to order Indian takeaway for a change. We hadn't had one in a very long time, and I was craving chicken Dansak. My kids mostly just eat the dip and the poppadums, and I pretend that means they're expanding their culinary palettes. Thankfully, one of them loves pilau rice, so she eats a little more than what amounts to crisps and dip. On this occasion, dinner costed ten pounds more than the last time I had ordered it and the kids ate a minimal amount. I ate as much as I could physically manage – still leaving half a curry and half a container of rice. I hate food waste. Maybe next time we get takeaway, we should stick with the kids' meals from the local chippy.

Anyway, even before that, it had been a costly day. One of my kids had attended a birthday party, so I had taken my other daughter for coffee (juice for her) and to buy clothes. I knew I'd have to rein it in for the rest of the week.

The following day, I decided we'd have a day at home to give my daughter's cough a chance to shift before school the next day. They suggested we start the day with microwave popcorn and a movie. We had Hocus Pocus downloaded from last year and the girls have decided since leaves are falling from trees, Halloween is upon us. So, we watched that, and everyone was perfectly content. However, as soon as the end credits started rolling, the requests kicked in. "Can we drive to McDonalds to get a milkshake?" my younger daughter pleaded.

"We haven't had one in ages. Pleaseeeeee."

"No, not today."

"Maybe we could get McDonald's for dinner?"

"We had takeaway last night."

"But we're sick," she whined. She'd recovered from her cold the previous week, and it hadn't impeded her going to her "BFF's" birthday party, but she knew it was a tool she could use on me.

"Not today, maybe another day."

"You know the way on my birthday we got milkshakes from Café Nero?" continued my older daughter. "Maybe we could order those. They brought them to the house – so we wouldn't even have to go out."

My memory was tasting my vanilla soya latte as she spoke and she was tempting me to give in to my own weakness for coffee, even though I had a perfectly functioning coffee maker, cafetiere, stovetop espresso maker and Vietnamese coffee press in the kitchen. It just wasn't the same as when someone else made it for you. I could feel the Café Nero caffeine and smoothly foamed milk coming to me in my mind, like a much-needed hug. But I resisted.

"Not today," I said.

"We'll discuss it later," my daughter said.

I realised the crazy contrast between that and the usage of the same expression in my own childhood. That was something I dreaded hearing, and that only came from the mouths of adults. It usually meant I was in for it when I got home.

I excused myself for a shower and the girls joined me upstairs within minutes, invading the bathroom and interrupting my shower with a running commentary.

"I can see you through the shower curtain, but not all of you – I can see your arms moving but that's it," said one of my kids.

I was used to such intrusion, so it was nothing new, but I still felt indignant about the fact I never got to shower alone. I just wanted to space out in the shower and clean myself in silence. I don't really know that I'm a great conversationalist at the best of times – but I'm certainly not in the shower. I snapped at everyone to hurry up and get out. It was the only time I've seen both my kids thoroughly washing and drying their hands, and I knew they were doing it on purpose, just to wind me up.

When I come out of the shower, I want to feel refreshed, but that rarely happens. I suppose the only good thing about that is that when it does, it means a lot more to me. It's only through living with the opposite to what you want that you can truly appreciate when you get your desire.

Back to the relentless requests – the girls followed me into my bedroom and jumped on the bed as I did my make-up. Sometimes I'm sure they wait for it to just have been changed, or at least neatly made, to start rebounding on it like kangaroos. I rushed through my make-up application, knowing my eyeliner was extra wiggly, but not having the will to redo it or to care. Before I had even finished my make-up, the girls started asking for a treat again. I always have to laugh when they work to present something I'm buying them as a favour they're doing for me.

"If we order it online now, it'll be here in fifteen minutes, and you can get your vanilla latte made for you. It's your favourite – isn't it?"

"You're tempting me now," I thought, but I didn't dare say it aloud.

That would be the same thing to them as placing an order then and there. I wanted to get them their milkshakes and God knows I always want a coffee shop delight, but on principal, I didn't want to buy them that day. We'd already been living outside our budget that weekend and I didn't want to spoil the girls too much either. The more they get, the more they feel entitled to ask for. It's a dangerous cycle – like whenever you call into a shop like Smyth's just to let them have a "quick look" (there is no such thing) and they end up with a trolley, filling it as you try to pull the toys from their grip, provoking tantrums that should have ended five years earlier. After the visit, even if they do get one of the items they wanted, they just start planning the next visit amongst themselves in the backseat on the car (before they've even got the new toys out of the packaging.) It's just like feeding an addiction. You have to cut it off at the source. That's why I so often get called "mean." I refuse to set foot in a toyshop with them. Entering one is just like savings account suicide. I somehow managed to bypass the delivery requests that day. They got absorbed in painting, and that always seems to do the trick. I made my own hot chocolate with marshmallows, so they were filled up with that, and I guess it satisfied their great need for a sweet treat – for that moment anyway.

Chapter Thirty-Six – Watching your Words

You have to be really careful about what you say in front of your kids. That feels like an obvious statement to make, but they really do soak it all in and spew it out again. My mum was telling my sister a story when my niece could still barely speak. It had the word "druggy" in it and my niece instantly picked the word up and repeated it over and over again. She had no idea what it meant, but she still used it with great confidence. It's highly likely in such a situation that your kid will repeat it once they start preschool, probably during their introduction to their new teacher.

I always have to watch what I say. I tend to swear without noticing I'm doing it – when I'm frustrated at least. I'm sure my kids have heard it all by now but thankfully, they don't say any of it themselves. I've recently realised that I need to be particularly careful in the car. Driving when people are doing dangerous things always makes me lose "the bap." "You arsehole," I'll shout. "You need to go back for driving lessons." If I let someone out and five cars proceed to follow them, I'll call them names and tell them to invite their family and friends to join all of them. I grew up with a mum with serious road rage and sometimes when I open my mouth, it comes out of me too. I just can't stand bad manners and bad behaviour and so much of it happens when you're out in the car.

Now, I notice my kids complaining about people's lack of manners, the fact someone wouldn't let us out, the fact someone was audacious enough not to wave when I let them out of a side street. I don't want to hear my own driving annoyance coming out of my kids, so I'm constantly having to check myself. But sometimes how they apply things they've heard you say are genuinely funny. I always complain about having to weave in and out on the motorway. I either have a racer harassing me from behind or a slow coach planted in front of me that has got the brake mixed up with the accelerator. We were driving along recently in a thirty-mile per hour zone and my daughter asked me, "Is that cyclist speeding?" I burst out laughing. She hears me complaining about cyclists constantly while I'm driving, so she's always on the lookout for them breaking the rules now, but she thought it was entirely possible that the guy was going forty in a thirty. He was pedalling along behind us, going fifteen at the most.

Sometimes, when they copy you and repeat what you've said, it's hilarious – especially when it's taken out of its original context, and it no longer makes sense. It's a great reminder to watch your words and I try to do that more and more. I also always walk on the school run because I know that would tip me over the edge and I'd be shouting obscenities in the car the entire time. When you walk with your kids, you get to enjoy their funny observations of the world around them anyway. As sentimental as it is – that's the material that makes precious memories.

Chapter Thirty-Seven – Poor Piñatas

My kids and I love a party, even though I can't face organising one with more than about ten people in attendance. We make our own little traditions every year and I get as excited about them as the girls do. It's strange how much they love the things I expect them to be disappointed with. One year, we had a really simple Halloween party with a couple of their friends, and I got a piñata. They'd been going on about it for a really long time and I finally caved and got them one. I never realised before just how many sweets it took to fill a piñata. It was like putting pound coins in a claw machine. Each time I dropped a packet in, it made a hollow sound. I didn't think there were anywhere near enough sweets inside it, but there were only going to be four kids involved, so I thought it wouldn't matter too much. The piñata came with a huge baton for breaking it open. It wasn't until after I'd filled it that I realised that I didn't have anywhere to hang it. How many people have a conveniently placed hook in the middle of a room? I thought about holding it myself, but I knew I'd just get clubbed instead of the donkey, or is it an alpaca? So, I improvised and hung it on the washing line. That seemed like it might work well, as long as I prayed for no rain that day.

When the kids arrived, they were elated, and I knew they were expecting a great party. I was nervous about whether I could deliver that, but they were easily pleased. We had some party food and make some Halloween crafts and then we went outside for piñata time. I watched them through the window, swinging the club at it. I'd always thought it was a bit of a brutal ritual. Maybe I was just lacking the background knowledge to understand how it had been born. But there was no denying the kids loved it, even if it was encouraging violence against (paper) animals. It held up much longer than I expected it to. The kids took good swings at it and showcased more strength than I'd known five years olds to be capable of. The animal was beheaded, the children cheered, and the sweets poured to the ground. The kids dropped to the floor, like they were trying to rescue riches that were pouring down a drain. I've always thought of piñatas as something that bring out the worst in people. Even if people aren't ordinarily overly selfish, they would trample on each other's heads to get that extra packet of sweets. And there is always one kid, without fail, that holds up their grossly greedy collection and shouts at the top their lungs that they got more than anyone else. Maybe that is why I haven't bought one since. I also just can't bear to see another animal beheaded – whether it is alive or not makes little difference to me. A week after the party, my family came over for dinner and my brother-in-law took a filled binbag outside to the bin for me. He came back inside carrying the club for the piñata.

"I found this lying in the middle of the back garden. Maybe it's not such a great idea leaving this lying out in plain sight. A burglar could easily break a window with that."

That hadn't even occurred to me, but when he pointed it out in his sensible way, it struck me how stupid it was of me to make such an oversight. If anyone broke into our house, they'd be disappointed with the results of their raid anyway. They'd get a TV from 2009, a laptop with a faulty keyboard and a dusty and stained coffee maker. Maybe I shouldn't advertise that, in case anyone reading this is really desperate for any of those items. I don't want to make anyone feel jealous either.

Another tradition of ours that my kids adore is when we go for a drive to see the Halloween or Christmas lights. In recent years, people are spending as much money on Halloween tat – I mean, décor - as they are on Christmas decorations. I love looking at those kinds of over the top, flashy lights. I still get excited about Christmas, and I love a light-up Santa on a roof as much as the next nutter. We do a little tour in the car and in advance of it, my kids and I bake iced cookies or gingerbread and they bring a travel cup with milk in it. I keep my energy levels up with my precious coffee. They sit and chat in the backseat, making crumbs everywhere and missing most of the major sights because they're so wrapped up in being out after dark and in competing for whoever has the most sprinkles – and if they've been evenly distributed. One silver ball is better currency than five strands of rainbow sprinkles – not that they would ever make that exchange or share them without a fist fight. I enjoy those simple things just as much as they do. There's nothing better than getting cosy in the Winter with a cup of hot chocolate under a blanket on the sofa and watching a nostalgic family film. More often than not, I fall asleep before we make it midway through, but that's part of the whole experience. My kids always laugh at me when I do that, and oddly, they seem to be comforted by my presence, even if I'm not conscious when I'm there. I remember my dad napping beside me and I found that comforting too. Maybe it reassures you that everything in your world is OK and that if the adults are relaxed, you can relax too. The only problem with this habit is that I fall asleep every time we go to the cinema now too. It usually depends on how well I've slept the night before and how boring the film is. The cinema provides the perfect conditions for a nap – dark room, silence apart from the background chatter from the screen, recliners, filling yourself up on snacks. I just hope no one else notices when I'm asleep. I struggle to stay awake during many kids' films, unless the plot really holds my attention. I've either seen them too many times, they're too predictable or I have so little interest in the plot's development that I'd rather dream up my own entertainment instead. Even if my eyes are slightly open, I still know when I'm asleep because my thoughts start making even less sense than they normally do. I start to mix reality and fiction together – and it isn't linked to the film. It's more like I see us sitting in our little row in the cinema seats and our pet koala is sitting next to my daughter too, and we are all eating liquorice, and no one is complaining about it. That truly would be fantastical.

Anyway – all our meaningful family traditions barely cost a thing: writing letters to Santa and posting them in a little post box I bought several years ago, painting pictures and making them sparkle with glitter, baking a batch of cookies and icing them together at the table, playing board games and drinking "champagne" (Schloer) out of wine glasses. The saying "the best things in life are free" might be one saccharine saying I can just about stomach, because there is truth in it. I still love an overpriced cup of coffee and a new dress that puts me over my budget sometimes though. Money can buy some good stuff – let's not discount that.

Chapter Thirty-Eight – Imperfect Timing

Embarrassment just comes along with being alive. I don't think it is something reserved for parenthood – unless you're one of those people that always manages to say the right thing, to never look clumsy and to always seem poised and perfect. I most definitely fall into the clumsy category. But sometimes, having kids increases your chance of encountering more embarrassing moments. Thankfully, since having kids, I find I care less and less what people think. Where someone's bad opinion of me would have previously slayed me, I react quickly and forget about it later that day. Maybe you just can't afford to hold onto as much of the humiliation because there are too many other things to think about. I can remember one particular day when we walked past a man with one leg. He looked completely independent and didn't look at all impeded nor bothered by his missing leg. But I don't know if that meant he'd see the humour in my kids pointing it out. In the middle of the busy street, my daughter shouted, "that man's leg is missing!" and pointed straight at him. He didn't seem to take us under his notice. Maybe it happens more often than you'd think, and other kids put their feet in their mouths too. (Maybe that was a poorly chosen expression.) But then my older daughter made it much worse. She completely freaked out at the sight of his stump. She started screeching. She was hysterical and she began to hyperventilate in a way I'd never seen her do before. It was clear that she was genuinely upset by the incident because she'd never seen it in real life before. I got a flashback to picking her up from school one day when she said they had watched a war-related video that day with a child in it that was an amputee. She seemed really troubled by that. I tried to shush her, inaudibly, and I gripped her hand more tightly, willing her to save her meltdown until the man was out of earshot, but she just kept going. I didn't know what his reaction was because I completely avoided eye contact. It was cowardly of me, but I didn't know to handle such a delicate situation. You can't say anything about disabilities anymore, without offending someone, and I say that as someone that, technically, has a disability. So, squawking, crying, and pointing just felt too complex to begin to deal with in the man's presence. Thankfully, she forgot about it as soon as we got home, but I doubt that poor man did.

That's something I've learnt about kids – they don't care about timing. There's no such thing as a bad moment for something in their worlds.

Chapter Thirty-Nine – Lessons Learned

I love the fact that kids have no real concept of time. I guess it's something they become burdened with through years of education and experience. Maybe if no one ever impressed this on us with timetables, we'd all be the same. Although, saying that, some adults have no concept of time and that isn't endearing. It usually means you're standing in the rain waiting for them and wondering if or when they're ever going to show up. With kids, it's cute though. They don't really plan for the future - unless my daughter stating with confidence that she plans to become a tooth fairy when she grows up counts. They do plan ahead, but only in terms of rewards – what they'd like for Christmas, how many houses we'll hit during trick or treating that Halloween, whose birthday is coming up next and what that means in terms of presents for the sibling. I try to live more like that too – worrying about the future doesn't help with anything. A lack of awareness of what's to come makes life easier. Even if the worst does end up happening – and it has to us – it rarely comes to you in as quick succession as the tsunami of worries in your mind. You can't pre-empt everything, so why try? My kids have really reminded me of this. I was swamped in worries before they came along. I'm still a natural worrier, but nowhere near as bad as I used to be.

The same applies to the past as to the future. My kids can't really grasp the concept of time or history. I remember that in my own childhood too. Every time we wrote about something more than ten years earlier, we began with "in the olden days." This phrase is never used in adulthood. Maybe it's because we have become one with the olden days by then. We'll have been born in them according to any written work our kids are composing in school anyway.

Recently, we were in the Ulster Transport Museum. It's a great place to take kids on a rainy day. I'm actually considering it now as I look out the window at torrential rain and regret booking the open farm for later today. There is a land, sea and sky gallery which I always remembered being a bit rubbish. We rarely ventured that far. It wasn't worth the extra few minutes of walking to get to the centre. But they've done it up recently and it has become my kids' favourite part. There is a green screen in it with a tractor, and another one with a jet ski. The kids love it, and they fight over whose turn it is the entire time we're there. As annoying as that is, it's usually a sign they've discovered something really special. They climb on board the tractor, or the jet ski and it shows them riding it on a screen in front of them. The whole thing is sort of implausible. At certain points, the tractor drives over houses, over the sea and through the sky. But that just adds to the hilarity of the experience. Anyway, after one of those visits, where it took me an age to pry them from the tractor and the jet ski, we went into the bicycle room. It has a collection of different bikes and trophies from races. At the doorway, stands a big penny farthing bike. I still don't know how people got onto them. You'd need a ladder to reach the seat – at least, I would, at five foot three. It just seems so impractical that I don't know why it was ever invented and how the idea was okayed with so many different manufacturers.

"There's a penny farthing," I said to my kids. I started to explain why it was called that, when my daughter interrupted me, looking at me earnestly.

"Is that the bike you used when you learned to ride a bike, Mummy?"

"I'm not that old," I laughed, suddenly feeling ancient. My children must have perceived me as such, I thought, to make a suggestion like that.

I laughed from my belly while she regarded me with confusion. She thought it was a perfectly ordinary question and couldn't see what had made me laugh.

That experience just highlights to me the fact that kids have a different concept of time to us. Anything is the past is regarded as historical, the future is like a fairyland where anything could happen and the present either drags on forever or flies by, depending on how satisfied they are with the programme of activities. Maybe in that respect, we, as adults, still experience the present in the same way.

In the end, we're all the same. Kids are just small people that come along as little reminders to us to stop and appreciate the things we've forgotten. They show us the joy to be found in jumping in the leaves, in stopping to say hi to a friendly cat, in drawing a picture and saying how proud we are of it. They remind us not to be modest to a fault, not to dwell on anything for too long and to remember the beauty of the physical world that surrounds us. It's easy as adults to get lost in our own heads and to forget to look outside the confines of our responsibilities and our assumptions. They give you a very loud wake-up call in every way – so long as you're prepared to take the time to listen and let them. Kids also put you in situations that are often mortifying at the time, but they're there to remind us of something important too, I think. They highlight the lack of control we have over our own worlds, our need to lighten up, to accept our imperfection and have a good old laugh at ourselves. Whatever mortification might come along with that is worth it in the end – even if you still grimace at its memory.

Printed in Great Britain
by Amazon

18625669R00098